DESCRIPTION OF IVAR'S COURSE DINNER

With any entree you choose on the Course Dinner you have your choice of cocktail and chowder and beverage. For cocktail your choice is crab, shrimp, Pacific oyster or juice; for chowder, Ivar's clam chowder, clam nectar or clam bisque; for beverage, coffee, tea, milk, or buttermilk. All desserts are extra.

FISH and FISHES

	A LA CARTE	COURSE DINNER
ALASKA HALIBUT STEAK	$1.35	$2.05
RED KING SALMON STEAK	1.55	2.25
GENUINE FINNAN HADDIE	1.00	1.70
PAN FRIED SMELT	.75	1.45
FILET OF SOLE, Grilled	.95	1.65
RED SNAPPER, Grilled	.95	1.65
BAKED SALMON FILET, Ivar's Dressing	1.25	1.95
PUGET SOUND SAND DAB (SOLE)	.95	1.65
PACIFIC SWORDFISH STEAK	1.45	2.15
RAINBOW TROUT, Pan Fried with Bacon, Fresh from Hatchery, Two Trout	1.85	2.55

CLAMS, OYSTERS, PRAWNS, SCALLOPS, CRAB, SHRIMP

FRIED LOUISIANA PRAWNS	1.55	2.25
FRENCH FRIED SCALLOPS	1.35	2.05
FRENCH FRIED CRAB LEGS	1.55	2.25
CREAMED CRAB or SHRIMP in CASSEROLE with Rice	1.50	2.20
CRAB or SHRIMP NEWBURG or AU GRATIN with Rice	1.60	2.30
COLD CRACKED CRAB (Half)	1.25	1.95
COLD CRACKED CRAB (Whole)	1.75	2.45
ACRES OF STEAMED CLAMS, Butter, Nectar	1.25	1.95
RAZOR CLAM FRY (Tasty, Maybe Tough)	1.50	2.20
ABALONE STEAK (Tender and Tasty)	1.80	2.50
ROCK POINT OYSTER FRY	1.10	1.80
OLYMPIA OYSTER FRY	2.35	3.05
OYSTER STEW, Rock Point 1.00 Olympia	1.75	

IVAR'S SPECIALTIES

FISH AND CHIPS, A PLENTY	.85	1.55
IVAR'S DE LUXE PUGET SHORE GRILL	1.75	2.45

(Salmon, Halibut, Sole, Oyster, Prawn, Crab Leg, Shrimp, Smelt, with French Fried Onion Rings.)

BEVERAGES and DESSERTS

COFFEE AND BUTTERMILK	.10
TEA AND MILK	.15
ICE CREAM AND SHERBET	.15
PIE	.20
SUNDAES	.35

AN IVAR BOOK OF BALLADS
from Puget Sound

Ask our cashier for this splendid illustrated souvenir . . . 12 of Ivar's fanciful ballads about fish and men, with piano music by George Frederick McKay. Only 50c in a big mailing envelope!

CLAM DIGGER ROOM

Have cocktails in a nautical atmosphere . . . or ask the waitress to serve you at your table. Wine and Liquor Menu also available.

You probably have heard about Ivar's International Pacific Free Style Amateur Clam Eating Contest Association, which sponsors one of the sporting events of the Pacific Northwest. In Ivar's Clam Bowl, a barge on Eliott Bay, contestants see how many steamed clams they can eat in 10 minutes. (Record-holder Joe Gagnon stowed 373.) The magnificent Clam Shell Crown is placed on the loaded victor by International Secretary of the I.P.F.S.A.C.E.C.A., Ivar Haglund, with the defeated candidates looking on hungrily, and every vantage point jammed with spectators.

SEAFOOD COOKBOOK

Ivar's

The O-fish-al Guide to Cooking the Northwest Catch

from **THE CREW AT IVAR'S**

SASQUATCH BOOKS
SEATTLE

Written, produced, printed, and shucked in the
United States of America
Published by Sasquatch Books
17 16 15 14 13   9 8 7 6 5 4 3 2

Photography: Jim Henkens
Food styling: Julie Hopper
Design: Anna Goldstein

Library of Congress Cataloging-in-Publication
Data is available.

ISBN: 978-1-57061-895-6
Sasquatch Books
1904 Third Avenue, Suite 710
Seattle, WA 98101
(206) 467-4300
www.sasquatchbooks.com
custserv@sasquatchbooks.com

CONTEST! How many food puns can you find in this cookbook?
Tell us at FoodPuns@KeepClam.com and you may win a surprise.

*To the past, present, and future
employees of Ivar's*

Ivar's chefs, testing new appetizers, from left to right: Juan Garcia, Steve Anderson, Craig Breedon, Phil Lam, Chris Garr, Einar Larson, May 2013. Still sailing: Ray Espinoza.

CONTENTS

Introduction   *11*

A BRIEF FISHTORY OF IVAR'S

How We Learned to Swim   *13*

75 Years of Unshellfish Leadership   *44*

Who Was Ivar Haglund?   *76*

A Seattle Favorite Since 1938   *125*

*Ivar's Today: Still Goofy
After All These Years*   *151*

Chapter 1: Appetizers   19

Jalapeño-Cilantro Marinated Prawns   23

Copper River Salmon Carpaccio
with Blood Orange Vinaigrette   24

Oysters Rockefeller   27

Dungeness Crab and Goat Cheese
Dip with Crostini   29

Ivar's Own Sports Illustrated
Geoduck Fritters   30

Dining Room Seafood Cocktail   33

Dungeness Crab Cakes   37

Mushrooms Stuffed with
Dungeness Crab   39

Sweet Grape Tomato Bruschetta   40

Wild Alaskan Salmon Sliders
with Kahlúa–Ancho Chile
Barbecue Sauce   43

Chapter 2: Salads, Soups & Chowders   49

Caesar Salad with Blackened Salmon   53

Bacon and Blue Knife-and-Fork Salad   57

Steve's Strawberry Caprese Salad   58

Grilled Halibut Salade Niçoise
with Three-Citrus Vinaigrette   61

Pink Banana Squash Soup   62

Dungeness Crab Bisque   63

Northwest Seafood Cobb Salad with
Hat Island Dressing   65

Ivar's Wild Alaskan Smoked
Salmon Chowder   67

Ivar's Famous Puget Sound
White Clam Chowder   68

Clamhattan Red Chowder   71

Einar's Viking Soup   72

Yellow Tomato Gazpacho   75

Chapter 3: Entrées   79

Sautéed Clams   82

Grilled Halibut Cheeks
with Cherry Chutney   83

Cedar-Plank Sockeye Salmon
with Hazelnut Vinaigrette   84

Possession Sound Seafood Stew   87

Blackened Lingcod with
Onion Rémoulade   89

Chris Garr's House-Made
    Bacon-Wrapped Halibut   90

Marsala-Steamed Mussels and Clams   93

Penn Cove Mussels in Thai Red
    Curry Broth   97

Poached Halibut with Lemon Dill Sauce   98

Breaded Razor Clams with
    Jalapeño-Ginger Tartar Sauce   99

Linguine with White Clam Sauce   101

Quilcene Oyster Pan Roast   102

Shrimp Newburg   103

Crab Louie with San Juan
    Island Dressing   104

Buttermilk-Fried Washington Smelt   109

Pan-Fried Trout with Apple
    Currant Chutney and Garr's
    House-Made Bacon   111

Copper River Penne Pasta with
    Marinara Cream Sauce   114

Alder-Grilled King Salmon   115

Grilled Copper River King Salmon with
    Champagne Tarragon Vinaigrette   118

Ivar's Crispy Fish Tacos   120

Fish-and-Chips Aplenty   123

Chapter 4: Sides & Staples   127

Garr's House-Made Bacon   131

Grays Harbor Cranberry Chutney   134

Apple Currant Chutney   135

Ivar's Original Cocktail Sauce   136

Ivar's Famous Tartar Sauce   137

Three-Cheese Polenta   138

Salmon House Mesquite
    Cornbread Muffins   141

Sautéed Spinach   142

Roasted Celery Root and
    Yukon Potato Hash   143

Brown Sugar–Roasted Acorn Squash   145

Ivar's Legendary Clam Nectar
    (Clam Stock)   146

Spicy Coleslaw   149

Roasted Fingerling Potatoes   150

Chapter 5: Desserts   153

Pecan Praline Bread Pudding with
    Bourbon Crème Anglaise   156

Four-Berry Crisp   158

Ranka's Accidentally the Best
    Carrot Cake   159

Ivar's Mukilteo Strawberry Shortcake   163

Stehekin Apple Cobbler   165

Triple Chocolate Cookie Sundae   167

What's the Best Catch? Suggested Menus   169

Acknowledgments   170

Index   171

Can you find the "mistake" in this photo? 1951, Pier 54. Write to us for the answer.

INTRODUCTION

If Seattle was part of your childhood, you shorely remember your first visit to Ivar's. You probably bellied up to the fish bar on Pier 54 after a trip to the aquarium, munching on fish-and-chips as folks did when Ivar's opened 75 years ago. You insisted on sitting outside in the drizzle so you could tease the seagulls, ignoring your parents' pleas to stay dry as your jeans soaked up water from the benches. Maybe you remember gazing at the Space Needle across Lake Union from Ivar's Salmon House, buttered cornbread warming your hand. By the time you visited Mukilteo Landing, a quick stop before the ferry to Whidbey Island, you were old enough to remember the fish: you ordered hot, crispy battered cod because you knew eating fish-and-chips wouldn't interfere with your ability to fight with your brother while wearing the kids' menu as a diver's mask. (Don't worry, it was designed for just that porpoise.)

Seattleites have early Ivar's memories because their parents ate there and still love to eat there too. On average, our customers visit our seafood bars about once every 10 days, so we take customer service seriously (at least, more seriously than we take most things). Those memories are what keep us swimming, working hard each day to provide you with the best fish and shellfish we can find and to serve it up in an environment that brings you back for more. After 75 years, we want Ivar's to remain a family experience, and we want it to be fun.

We also want it to be delicious. So far, we're skating by. Ivar's receives boatloads of recipe requests, and every week we respond, just as Ivar used to do. To celebrate our 75th anniversary, we've reeled in a collection of recipes both old and new, a net full of chefs' favorites and old reliables that keep our restaurants and seafood bars afloat. We've tested them in professional kitchens and home kitchens and in some motor home kitchens, so no matter what boat you're in, our recipes work.

Ivar Haglund, our flounder, had an exuberant comic spirit—one we try to keep alive with us in everything we do (hence our slogan, "Keep Clam"). Peppered among the recipes, you'll find the fish tales that have gotten people steamed up over the years, like the story about Ivar's underwater billboards and the government drama behind Ivar's notorious clam stamp. We hope you'll enjoy this book as a guide to re-creating our piscatorial pleasures in your own kitchen, and also as a leisurely, entertaining swim through Ivar's history. Because for the crew at Ivar's today—like for Ivar Haglund—nothing beats a finny story.

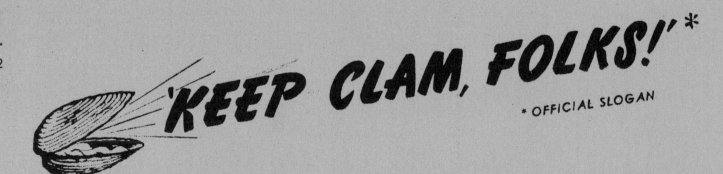

"KEEP CLAM, FOLKS!"*

*OFFICIAL SLOGAN

HOW WE LEARNED TO SWIM

Ivar Haglund, our flounder, liked to say that Ivar's started because of one thing: hunger. But it really started with a guitar and an aquarium.

Born in West Seattle in 1905, Ivar Haglund was raised by a single father who praised little (he was a bit of a snapper), but always recognized Ivar's sense of humor. From an early age, Ivar was an entertainer, crooning for anyone who wanted to listen. In college, he made money singing, dancing, and playing the ukulele or guitar, often all at once. After graduating from the University of Washington in 1928 with a degree in economics—an ironic degree to earn a year before the stock market crash of 1929, but Ivar was always ahead of the times—Ivar lived off money from his late father's rental properties and enjoyed a bohemian lifestyle, writing folk songs and playing guitar. He developed a decent reputation as a Western folk singer, keeping company with the likes of Pete Seeger, Burl Ives, and Woody Guthrie.

Inspired by several visits to Seaside, Oregon, where his cousins operated a profitable aquarium, Ivar opened a small aquarium on Harbor Avenue in West Seattle in 1937, with specimens he gathered off Alki Point under a special permit from the city.

Finding limited success, the next year Ivar moved his little dime aquarium to Pier 54, which in those days was Pier 3. (The Navy renumbered Seattle's piers during World War II because its ships couldn't seem to keep up with Seattle's odd numbering system.) He used his musical prowess to promote his business by singing ballads and chanteys on daily radio shows. Then, as now, the pier was a waterfront attraction in the summer, but early winter has never been a fabulous time to be out meandering in Seattle weather, and Ivar didn't have a huge advertising budget when business slowed down. So in December 1940, he pulled the first of what would be many big publicity stunts: a few days before Christmas, he put Patsy, the aquarium's new baby seal, into a baby buggy, and took her (him, actually) to see Santa Claus at Frederick & Nelson, then one of the largest Seattle department stores. By the time Ivar had traveled with Patsy from the pier to the line for Santa,

Ivar Haglund, 1945.

Patsy the Seal visiting Santa, December 1940.

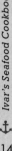
word had spread. They were greeted by one surprised Santa Claus and groupers of journalists and reporters—proof for Ivar (and for Frederick & Nelson) that traditional media weren't always the most beneficial for a company. From then on, when it came to garnering press for his various endeavors, Ivar depended on his own ingenuity.

In the 1940s Pier 3 was owned by the Washington Fish and Oyster Company (today a part of Ocean Beauty Seafoods). Since fishing boats (with a large percentage of the Pacific Northwest's annual harvest) unloaded there, it seemed like a natural spot for a fish bar. Fellow West Seattle High School graduates Jack and Frank Alger, who had started Alki's Spud Fish and Chips in 1935, taught Ivar a few things about fish-and-chips. Soon after, in conjunction with two other West Seattle friends, Ivar set up a hole-in-the-wall fish-and-chips stand near the aquarium, called, simply, "The Shop." They sold drinks from a cooler and fish to passersby, but Ivar noted that his aquarium customers wanted a place to sit down to eat. The fish-and-chips spot had threatened to put Steve's, another restaurant on the pier, out of business. And by then, Ivar had a fine kettle of fish in his collection, but food sales had begun to outweigh his aquarium income. So in 1946, with encouragement from his father-in-law and a loan he probably shouldn't have qualified for, Ivar Haglund sold the aquarium and opened Acres of Clams, a restaurant devoted to piscatorial pleasures of the edible variety. (And no, he never did cook up any of the fish from his aquarium. Didn't have the gull.)

Although the first few days were roughy (Haglund didn't even have enough change to run his cash register), Ivar's Acres of Clams succeeded, in part because of its name. It mimics the last few lines of "The Old Settler," a song credited to Pete Seeger (but one that, some argue, may have been inspired by Ivar Haglund):

> *No longer a slave of ambition*
> *I laugh at the world and its shams*
> *As I think of my happy condition—*
> *Surrounded by acres of clam-m-m-s!*

Because Ivar, by then a musician well known on the radio, performed the song often, the name had immediate appeal and recognition.

The original Ivar's was a fine-dining experience, serving dishes such as Lobster Thermidor and Oysters Rockefeller. Servers wore starched skirts; diners wore dresses and ties. But then, as now, Acres of Clams was more than just a restaurant, bar, and seagull-watching station. It was and is also a maritime museum. From carved mermaids and Japanese glass fishing floats to a detailed model of each fireboat in Seattle's history, every corner of the space is filled with relics, including that guy sitting in booth 27. We credit the collection in part to Ivar's insatiable curiosity for all things nautical, but also to his realization that in the 1940s, people didn't eat out very often. Having additional "entertainment" in the form of kitschy décor (like his grandmother's china collection) made people feel like they were getting their money's worth. Making the place a little corny also enabled customers to feel a bit superior to their surroundings, and hence more relaxed. And really, who doesn't love a clam gun collection?

As the restaurant's popularity grew, so did Ivar's reputation as a stuntman. When a railroad tank car filled with corn syrup flooded the train tracks near the restaurant, Ivar immediately asked the chef at Acres of Clams to make a stack of giant pancakes. Next, Ivar donned a pair of waders, walked into the middle of the spill, and ladled the syrup over hot pancakes, assuring onlookers that Ivar's doesn't skimp on syrup (or anything else, for that matter). He launched a yearly clam-eating contest, East Coast versus West Coast, garnering national media attention. (The media probably also liked seeing the scantily clad royalty—a Princess Little Neck and a Miss Halibut Cheeks—elected every year too.)

Ivar Haglund was not the type of fish who swam backward; he was always looking for his next project. In 1951 he opened Ivar's on Broadway, a drive-in restaurant that lasted 19 years (and also happened to serve Mexican food, Chinese food, and pizza—perhaps the first food court in the country). In 1956 he opened Ivar's Fifth Avenue, on Seattle's Fifth Avenue, which later became known as The Captain's Table and eventually moved to Elliott Avenue. In 1964 Ivar began the Fourth of Jul-Ivar's fireworks, a community fireworks display that carried on until 2008. In 1966 he purchased Pier 54, where his first restaurant was located, for half a million dollars and started calling Acres of Clams the "Ivar-y Coast." Soon after, he opened Ivar's Salmon House at the north end of Lake Union—a concession to his original plan, which had

Ivar scooping syrup from the spill onto pancakes.

been to open a floating Roman bathhouse in Seattle's Ballard neighborhood.

In 1980 he opened his first quick-service restaurant, in Ballard, acquiring employees Dave Fechter and Paul Lawson, who still work for Ivar's today. Thirteen other quick-service spots soon followed, each replacing an Arthur Treacher's Fish & Chips restaurant.

Ivar Haglund passed away in January 1985, at 79 years old, of a heart attack. But even without leadership from its flounder—or more accurately, because of it—the Ivar's restaurants flourished. That same year, emerging from a remodel, Ivar's Acres of Clams branded its "Keep Clam" slogan, now a phrase associated with Ivar's by visitors across the globe. In 1992 Ivar's purchased Taylor's Landing and renamed it Ivar's Mukilteo Landing, to replace the Captain's Table. (Mukilteo means "the gathering place.") Two years later, Ivar's famous original clam chowder became available in grocery stores around the country—and later in Japan, China, Canada, and Mexico.

Since then, Ivar's has opened at Husky Stadium, Safeco Field, CenturyLink Field, Key Arena, Cheney Stadium, and at Sea-Tac Airport, and now operates about 30 seafood bars.

Every year, Ivar's sells almost 2 million orders of cod-and-chips—more if you count halibut, sole, salmon, shrimp, and clams, of course. It still makes headlines for its wacky stunts, like discovering billboards under Puget Sound (see page 139 for the whole story) and celebrating its centennial 28 years early. If you ask us, that's a pretty good run.

"The James Beard Foundation ought to create a new category for restaurateurs who help their cities hold on to a sense of humor. A trickster like Ivar would be the perfect choice."
—KNUTE BERGER FOR *SEATTLE MAGAZINE*, APRIL 2010

Dan Salldin painting the pier.

Ivar after purchasing Smith Tower, 1976.

CHAPTER 1
APPETIZERS

Snacks and bites to hook your appetite

Jalapeño-Cilantro Marinated Prawns   23

Copper River Salmon Carpaccio
with Blood Orange Vinaigrette   24

Oysters Rockefeller   27

Dungeness Crab and Goat Cheese
Dip with Crostini   29

Ivar's Own Sports Illustrated
Geoduck Fritters   30

Dining Room Seafood Cocktail   33

Dungeness Crab Cakes   37

Mushrooms Stuffed with
Dungeness Crab   39

Sweet Grape Tomato Bruschetta   40

Wild Alaskan Salmon Sliders with Kahlúa–Ancho
Chile Barbecue Sauce   43

*I*n the beginning, appetizers at Ivar's were quite simple, just bites to wet the appetite. As tastes evolved and diners began spending more money eating out, the restaurant's beautiful but uncomplicated starters, like poached shrimp dipped happily in Ivar's Original Cocktail Sauce (page 136) or fresh oysters served on the half shell, gave way to more intricate dishes, like classic Oysters Rockefeller. Today, the menu boasts a mouthwatering combination of classics—the Rockefeller is now made with sambuca and Garr's House-Made Bacon (page 131)—and we offer more contemporary appetizers, like Wild Alaskan Salmon Sliders with Kahlúa–Ancho Chile Barbecue Sauce.

Of course, it's important to flex your mussels right from the start when you're making a meal for someone for the first time, and every dinner companion likes different things. The seafood connoisseur will appreciate the Copper River Salmon Carpaccio with Blood Orange Vinaigrette, whose ultra-thin slivers of two types of salmon make even the most experienced fish lover pause to appreciate the difference between king and sockeye. For anemone (or a buddy who also loves spicy food), cook Jalapeño-Cilantro Marinated Prawns using habañero peppers, and watch your competition sweat. If you want a steamer of an evening, you'll need to start with Ivar's Own Sports Illustrated Geoduck Fritters—just make sure your dining companion is there for the entire preparation process.

If you're just off the boat, try the Mushrooms Stuffed with Dungeness Crab—they're a staff favorite.

Jalapeño-Cilantro Marinated Prawns

Marinated in a piquant mixture of cilantro, lime juice, hot peppers, and garlic, these grilled shrimp are a summer favorite. Eat them right off the skewers or, for a larger meal, add them to tacos. Remember: Don't eat the skewers.

SERVES 4

1. To make the marinade, in a blender, combine all the ingredients and blend until very smooth. Pour into a medium bowl and add the prawns. Toss, pick up off the floor, cover, and marinate in the refrigerator overnight or up to 2 days.

2. Preheat a gas or charcoal grill to high heat. Skewer the prawns and grill for 3 to 4 minutes per side, or until marked and just cooked through. Serve hot, with a twinkle in your eye.

SPECIAL EQUIPMENT: 8 bamboo or metal skewers (if using bamboo, submerge in water and soak for 30 minutes before using)

FOR THE MARINADE:

1 bunch cilantro, stems trimmed

⅓ cup canola or other vegetable oil

2½ tablespoons extra-virgin olive oil

4 teaspoons finely grated lime zest (from 2 medium limes)

4 tablespoons freshly squeezed lime juice (from 2 medium limes)

1½ large jalapeño or habanero peppers, seeded and chopped

6 cloves garlic, smashed and peeled

2½ tablespoons honey

1½ teaspoons sea salt

1½ teaspoons freshly ground black pepper

· · · · · · ·

1½ pounds jumbo prawns (24 to 30), peeled and deveined, with tails left on

Sabrie and Gerry Evans aboard the Washington State Ferry Walla Walla.

Copper River Salmon Carpaccio with Blood Orange Vinaigrette

The secrets to making a beautiful salmon carpaccio are simple: keep the fish cold and use a sharp knife. We recommend using salmon pieces of even thickness (ask your fishmonger for a chunk from the head end of a fillet, and make sure it's from a source you trust, because you'll be eating it raw). To make slicing easier, wrap the fish in plastic wrap and freeze it for about 30 minutes, until it just starts to firm up, then unwrap and cut it with a very sharp knife.

SERVES 4

3 blood oranges

½ fennel bulb, shaved paper thin

3 cups mixed baby greens

FOR THE VINAIGRETTE:

¼ cup freshly squeezed blood orange juice (from about 3 blood oranges)

¼ cup unseasoned rice vinegar

2 teaspoons honey

¼ cup extra-virgin olive oil

Sea salt

Pinch of freshly ground white pepper

• • • • • • •

4 ounces Copper River king salmon

4 ounces Copper River sockeye salmon

Freshly ground black pepper

1. With a sharp knife, cut the peel and pith from the oranges. Carefully cut the oranges into thin slices and place in a medium bowl. Add the fennel and greens and set aside.

2. For the vinaigrette, in a blender, combine the blood orange juice, vinegar, honey, oil, salt to taste, and white pepper, and blend until well combined.

3. With a very sharp, thin-bladed knife, slice the salmon very thinly and arrange on plates. Toss the orange and greens mixture with 3 to 4 tablespoons of the vinaigrette. Place the salad in the middle of the plated salmon, season to taste with black pepper and more salt, and drizzle with more vinaigrette. Serve immediately.

It's best to use a mandoline to cut the fennel. Also, if you can't get blood oranges, substitute navel or Cara Cara oranges and add a touch of lemon juice to the vinaigrette (Meyer lemons are great if you can find them). Finally, if you can't find both king and sockeye salmon, keep clam and just use ½ pound of one type.

Oysters Rockefeller

Invented by the New Orleans restaurant Antoine's in 1899, Oysters Rockefeller was named for the famously wealthy family because each bite is almost indecently rich. Our version, made with our own bacon, cream, spinach, and sambuca, is no exception—and it's a good way to remember that even if you don't have a world-renowned surname, the world can still be your oyster.

SERVES 2 TO 4

1. Cook the bacon in a large skillet (preferably generations-old cast iron) in your cabin on Henry Island (or over a beach fire) over medium-high heat until crisp. Remove with a slotted spoon and discard all but 2 tablespoons of the fat, leaving 1 tablespoon in the pan and reserving 1 tablespoon in a bowl. Add the garlic to the pan and cook for 30 seconds. Taste the sambuca. (Two glasses should be sufficient.) If it's good (make sure), add the 3 tablespoons of sambuca and cook until it reduces to a thick syrup, about 1 minute. Stir in the Worcestershire, hot sauce, and cream and bring to a simmer. Simmer until very thick, stirring occasionally, about 1 to 2 minutes. Pour into a bowl and set aside.

2. Add the reserved tablespoon of bacon fat to the same skillet. Add the spinach and cook until wilted, about 2 minutes. (Drink another glass of sambuca while you wait.) Finely chop and stir the spinach into the cream mixture along with the bacon. Season to taste with salt and pepper.

3. In a small bowl, combine the panko and Parmesan and set aside.

4. Preheat the oven to 450 degrees F. Shuck the oysters and lay each in its bottom shell on a baking sheet lined with the salt (use enough to keep the oysters from tipping over). Top each with 1 tablespoon of the spinach mixture and sprinkle with a scant ½ teaspoon of the panko mixture. Bake for 7 to 9 minutes, or until the panko is browned and the spinach mixture is bubbling. Transfer to plates, sprinkle with the parsley, and serve.

4 ounces store-bought or Garr's House-Made Bacon (page 131), diced

4 large cloves garlic, minced

3 tablespoons sambuca or other anise-flavored liqueur, plus additional for tasting

2 teaspoons Worcestershire sauce

½ teaspoon hot sauce

⅓ cup heavy cream

2 packed cups baby spinach

Kosher salt and freshly ground black pepper

3 tablespoons panko bread crumbs

3 tablespoons grated Parmesan

1 dozen oysters

1 tablespoon chopped fresh flat-leaf parsley

Aw Shucks

Shucking oysters isn't so hard, as long as you're patient. And an oyster knife helps. To open an oyster, line the palm of your nondominant hand with a folded kitchen towel. (If you're an economist, use your third hand.) Hold the oyster in that hand, hinge facing you, with the flattest side of the oyster up. Hold the oyster knife in your dominant hand (hold the handle, not the blade) and press the hinge of the oyster down onto the blade, wiggling the blade, if necessary, to pry the oyster open. When the shell pops open, side the blade under the flat side of the shell, loosening the oyster muscle from the upper shell. Discard the flat side of the shell, then serve the oysters raw (try to keep as much of that yummy juice as possible) or use for Oysters Rockefeller. If you find a pearl, give it to your mother. She'll shorely appreciate it.

Sammy Woo, expert shucker at Ivar's since 1975.

Dungeness Crab and Goat Cheese Dip with Crostini

If you dine with Ivar's president Bob Donegan, your meal comes with free eating advice. Bob is known for saying, "Eat slowly. Don't stop." Here's a classic crab dip that puts his words to good use. When it comes out of the kitchen, it's usually too piping hot to eat on turbot speed, but the combination of fresh Dungeness, minced jalapeño, and goat cheese makes it irresistible. When you make it at home, you can perhaps edit his mantra to, "Start slowly. Don't stop."

Of course, if you want to fish it out of the dish with tortilla chips or pita bread for breakfast in the morning, straight from the refrigerator, we won't judge you.

SERVES 4 TO 6

1. Preheat the oven to 450 degrees F. In a large bowl, mix together the cream and goat cheeses until well blended. Add the mayonnaise, bell pepper, shallot, garlic, jalapeño, scallion, lemon juice, Worcestershire sauce, egg yolk, cayenne, and crab. Mix well, season with salt and pepper to taste, and transfer to a small, shallow baking dish (1 quart) or pie plate.

2. In another bowl, combine the panko and Parmesan and sprinkle over the crab mixture. Bake until lightly browned and bubbling, about 8 to 10 minutes. Sprinkle with the parsley and serve with the crostini and grapes. Breathe between bites.

½ cup softened cream cheese

⅓ cup goat cheese (not mountain goat, please)

3 tablespoons mayonnaise

⅓ cup finely diced red bell pepper

1 tablespoon minced shallot

1 clove garlic, minced

1½ teaspoons minced jalapeño

1 scallion, minced (scallion, not scallop)

1 tablespoon freshly squeezed lemon juice (Meyer preferred)

1 tablespoon Worcestershire sauce

1 large egg yolk

Pinch of cayenne pepper

1 pound picked-over cooked Dungeness crabmeat, drained

Kosher salt and freshly ground black pepper

¼ cup panko bread crumbs

¼ cup finely grated Parmesan

1 tablespoon chopped fresh flat-leaf parsley

Thinly sliced artisan bread, toasted (aka crostini)

28 red grapes

Frank lands a big king salmon off Alki Point.

Ivar's Own Sports Illustrated Geoduck Fritters

Originally published alongside an interview of Ivar Haglund in a 1964 issue of *Sports Illustrated* magazine, this recipe is a go-to for anyone who wants to start good conversation before dinner.

SERVES 4 TO 6

1 cup sifted all-purpose flour

1 teaspoon baking powder

1 teaspoon ground nutmeg

1 teaspoon kosher salt

2 large eggs, beaten

1 cup milk

2 teaspoons grated onion

1 tablespoon unsalted butter, melted

2 cups finely chopped or ground geoduck (store-bought, or from a roughly 2-pound geoduck)

Canola or other vegetable oil for frying

Serve these with Ivar's Famous Tartar Sauce (page 137) or lemon wedges (Meyer preferred).

1. In a large bowl, whisk together the flour, baking powder, nutmeg, and salt. In a shallow bowl mix together the eggs, milk, onion, and butter. Stir the wet ingredients into the dry ones and mix just until combined. Stir in the geoduck and set the batter aside.

2. Line a baking sheet with paper towels. Heat about 3 inches of the oil in a fryer or Dutch oven over high heat until it registers 350 degrees F on a deep-fat thermometer. Using two tablespoons, carefully deposit the dough in tablespoon-sized balls into the oil in batches of 4 or 6, depending on the size of your pan, turning, for 2 to 3 minutes each batch, or until dark golden brown on the outside. Do not crowd the fritters (this is not a mosh pit), keep turning them, and keep the oil at 350 degrees F. Remove to the prepared baking sheet to drain, then serve. Chew well. Smile broadly.

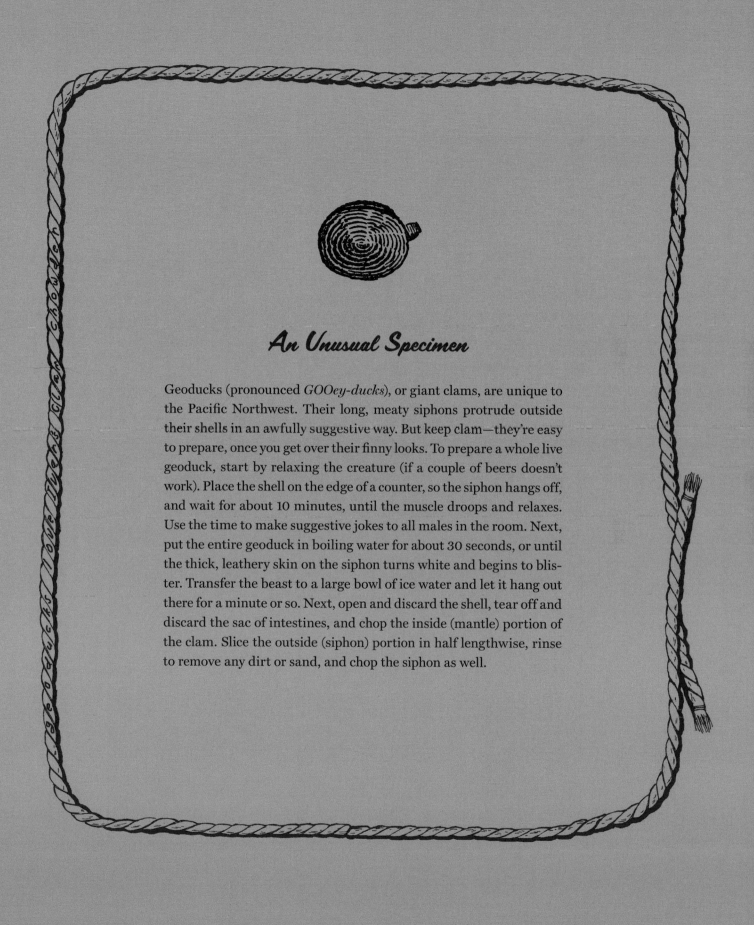

An Unusual Specimen

Geoducks (pronounced *GOOey-ducks*), or giant clams, are unique to the Pacific Northwest. Their long, meaty siphons protrude outside their shells in an awfully suggestive way. But keep clam—they're easy to prepare, once you get over their finny looks. To prepare a whole live geoduck, start by relaxing the creature (if a couple of beers doesn't work). Place the shell on the edge of a counter, so the siphon hangs off, and wait for about 10 minutes, until the muscle droops and relaxes. Use the time to make suggestive jokes to all males in the room. Next, put the entire geoduck in boiling water for about 30 seconds, or until the thick, leathery skin on the siphon turns white and begins to blister. Transfer the beast to a large bowl of ice water and let it hang out there for a minute or so. Next, open and discard the shell, tear off and discard the sac of intestines, and chop the inside (mantle) portion of the clam. Slice the outside (siphon) portion in half lengthwise, rinse to remove any dirt or sand, and chop the siphon as well.

Dining Room Seafood Cocktail

It's not an accident that the décor in Ivar's restaurants is hoki; our flounder planned it that way. The way he saw it, customers would be happiest with their meal if they were as comfortable eating at Ivar's as they were at home. So rather than sprinkle a menu with words that made diners feel like they were in French class, Ivar made things silly. As he used to ask, who could be intimidated by a menu that looks like a clam? Ironically, the corny décor and cartoonish menu also allowed him to sneak in ingredients that were, at the time, quite unfamiliar to diners, like the avocado in this seafood cocktail.

SERVES 4

1. In a large saucepan or Dutch oven over high heat, bring the water, the juice of the lemon halves and the halves themselves, thyme sprigs, pickling spice, and salt to a boil. Reduce the heat, cover, and simmer for 5 minutes. Stir in the medium shrimp and cook for 2 minutes, or just until the shrimp are opaque in the center. Drain the shrimp in a colander, rinse under cold running water, dry on paper towels, and refrigerate, tightly covered, until thoroughly chilled, about 60 minutes.

2. Arrange the chilled shrimp and bay shrimp, crab, and avocado on 4 plates. Put the cocktail sauce in a small bowl, sprinkle it with the horseradish, and serve with the chilled shellfish.

½ gallon water (1.89 litres if you are Canadian, or a scientist)

1 large lemon, halved (Meyer preferred)

5 sprigs fresh thyme

1 tablespoon pickling spice

1 tablespoon kosher salt

24 medium shrimp (about 1 pound), peeled and deveined

14 ounces cooked baby bay shrimp

4 ounces cooked Dungeness crabmeat, drained (unless you're serving sea otters, please remove all the shell pieces)

1 ripe avocado, peeled, seeded, and thinly sliced

1 cup Ivar's Original Cocktail Sauce (page 136) or other cocktail sauce

4 teaspoons finely grated fresh horseradish, or prepared horseradish to taste

Ivar's

A La Carte

COCKTAILS AND APPETIZERS

CRAB OR SHRIMP COCKTAIL	SMALL .35, LARGE	.65
QUILCENE OYSTER COCKTAIL	SMALL .50, LARGE	.80
OLYMPIA OYSTER COCKTAIL	SMALL .65, LARGE	1.00
TOMATO OR GRAPEFRUIT JUICE		.20
CRAB LEG COCKTAIL		1.00

SANDWICHES AND SNACKS

CREAMED CRAB ON TOAST	.90
CREAMED SHRIMP ON TOAST	.90
OYSTER SANDWICH	.90
TUNA FISH SANDWICH	.50
GRILLED CHEESE SANDWICH	.45

SALADS AND LOUIES

CRAB LOUIE DUNGENESS	1.25
ALASKA SHRIMP LOUIE	1.25
COMBINATION CRAB AND SHRIMP SALAD	1.25
COMBINATION SEAFOOD SALAD	.85

CHOWDER-NECTAR-SOUP

IVAR'S FAMOUS CLAM CHOWDER FROM FRESH CLAMS WITH NECTAR BASE

CUP .15, BOWL .25, COLOSSAL BOWL			.35
SUPER COLOSSAL BOWL			.65

Ivar's Clam Nectar Same Price as Above. Cream Clam Bisque, Made with Minced Razor Clams and Milk, Same Price as Above.

BEVERAGES AND DESSERTS

COFFEE, MILK, BUTTERMILK	.10
POT OF TEA	.15
PIE OR ICE CREAM	.15
CAKE	.20
SUNDAES	.25

Seafood from the cold waters of the Pacific, Alaska and the Bering Sea is the World's finest. We take pride in preparing and serving it to you.

Ivar Haglund

For Sea Food to Take Home, Stop at Ivar's Famous Fish Bar in Front!

Not responsible for loss of personal property. We reserve right of seating patrons.

Our seafoods are cooked to order. Some of them require 15 to 20 minutes time for proper preparation. Please ask us if you have any questions.

Welco
where
cult

On
foot
Mad

YOUR *Course Dinners* **INCLUDE**

Choice of One Cocktail or Juice
Choice of One Chowder or Nectar or Soup

ENTREE A La Carte Portion   **BEVERAGE** Coffee, Tea or Milk

All Desserts Extra

Acres of Clams

		A LA CARTE	COURSE DINNER
FISH!	ALASKA HALIBUT STEAK	1.25	1.75
	RED KING SALMON STEAK	1.25	1.75
	FRIED SMELT	.65	1.15
FISH!	FRIED FILET OF SOLE	.85	1.35
	BAKED SALMON FILET IVAR'S DRESSING	1.25	1.75
CLAMS! CLAMS!	ACRE OF STEAMED CLAMS, BUTTER, CUP OF NECTAR	1.00	1.50
	RAZOR CLAM FRY (TASTY BUT MAYBE TOUGH)	1.50	2.00
	ABALONE STEAK (TENDER)	1.80	2.30
OYSTERS! OYSTERS!	QUILCENE OYSTER FRY	1.00	1.50
	OLYMPIA OYSTER FRY	1.75	2.25
	OYSTER STEW QUILCENE .85, OLYMPIA 1.25		
Ivar's Specialties—	FISH AND CHIPS, PLENTY	.85	1.35
	IVAR'S DE LUXE SHORE GRILL . . . (Salmon, Halibut, Sole, Prawns, Oyster, Crab, Shrimp, Smelt with French Fried Onion Rings)	1.65	2.15
Special Seafood Barbecues	IVAR'S BARBECUED FISH AND CHIPS (OUR OWN ORIGINAL)	1.00	1.50
	BARBECUED PRAWNS	1.40	1.90
	BARBECUED OYSTERS	1.30	1.80
	BARBECUED CRAB LEGS	1.30	1.80
	BARBECUED CRACKED CRAB	1.85	2.35
PRAWNS	FRIED LOUISIANA PRAWNS	1.35	1.85
SCALLOPS	FRENCH FRIED SCALLOPS	1.25	1.75
	FRENCH FRIED CRAB LEGS	1.25	1.75
CRAB	COLD CRACKED CRAB (HALF)	.85	1.35
	COLD CRACKED CRAB (WHOLE)	1.50	2.00
SHRIMP	CREAMED CRAB, OR SHRIMP IN CASSEROLE WITH RICE	1.30	1.80

MEAT AND CHICKEN

	A LA CARTE	COURSE DINNER
FRIED SPRING CHICKEN TO ORDER	1.65	2.15
SELECT SIRLOIN STEAK	2.00	2.50
BREADED VEAL CUTLET, GRAVY	1.15	1.65

Ivar's Acres of Clams menu, circa 1950.

Dungeness Crab Cakes

When it comes to crab cakes, Ivar's has a simple goal: they should taste like the sweet, flaky Dungeness crab that gives them their name. With that in mind, we add only enough other stuff to hold the crab cakes together. Serve them as is, with a squeeze of fresh lemon or Ivar's Famous Tartar Sauce (page 137). Don't use them as hockey pucks—they're not strong enough to stay together on the ice.

SERVES 6

1. Preheat the oven to 200 degrees F. Line a baking sheet with several layers of paper towels.

2. Whisk the egg in a medium bowl. Whisk in the mayonnaise, scallion, bell pepper, lemon juice, and Old Bay. Add the crab and the panko; season to taste with salt and pepper. Mix with your hands until the mixture holds it shape when gently squeezed together. Make each crab cake with a level measuring tablespoon's worth of the mixture, pressing the crab tightly together and forming balls with your hands, then flattening them slightly into ½-inch-thick pucks. Place the additional panko on a plate and roll the cakes in breadcrumbs to coat completely.

3. Heat the oil in a large skillet over medium-high heat until it registers 375 degrees F on a deep-fry thermometer. Cook the crab cakes in batches, turning to cook all sides, for 2 to 4 minutes each batch, or until light golden brown and crisp. Do not crowd the crab cakes; keep them turning, and keep the oil at 375 degrees F. With a slotted spoon, remove the crab cakes, place them on the prepared baking sheet, and keep them warm in the oven while you cook the rest. Serve hot.

1 large egg

⅓ cup mayonnaise

2 tablespoons finely chopped scallion

2 tablespoons finely chopped red bell pepper

2 teaspoons freshly squeezed lemon juice (Meyer preferred)

1¼ teaspoons Old Bay seasoning

1 pound picked-over cooked Dungeness crabmeat, drained

¾ cup panko bread crumbs, plus additional 1 cup for coating

Kosher salt and freshly ground black pepper

3 cups canola or other vegetable oil

Mushrooms Stuffed with Dungeness Crab

Start with a crab-heavy stuffing reminiscent of a crab cake but enriched with mascarpone cheese. Stuff it into the world's luckiest white mushrooms, drizzle it with a sweet homemade carrot oil, and you've got one of Ivar's best-selling appetizers. Pop them into your mouth whole, if you've got the gull. Just don't forget to chew.

SERVES 4

1. To make the carrot oil, preheat the oven to 350 degrees F. Stir the carrots and oil together in a small loaf pan; season to taste with salt and pepper. Roast for 45 minutes, or until the carrots are very soft. Let cool to room temperature. Puree in a blender and add more salt and pepper to taste.

2. To make the stuffing, in a large bowl, whisk together the mascarpone, egg white, lemon juice, Worcestershire, Old Bay, salt, and hot sauce to taste. Stir in the scallions, bell pepper, and parsley. Stir in the crab and panko; taste and adjust seasoning. Refrigerate, covered, for at least 1 hour before using.

3. Preheat the broiler. Fill each mushroom cap with the crab mixture and place on a broiler pan or baking sheet. Broil for 10 to 12 minutes, until browned and heated through. Transfer to a platter, top each mushroom with a tiny drizzle of carrot oil and a pinch of parsley, and serve hot.

You can also use a combination of Dungeness and snow crabmeats, if you prefer. You'll do best to make two or three batches. Everyone loves 'em, and no one can eat just one. Eat slowly, don't stop.

FOR THE CARROT OIL:

1 medium carrot, grated

½ cup canola or other vegetable oil

Kosher salt and freshly ground black pepper

FOR THE STUFFING:

⅓ cup mascarpone cheese

1 large egg white

1½ teaspoons freshly squeezed lemon juice (Meyer preferred)

½ teaspoon Worcestershire sauce

¼ teaspoon Old Bay seasoning (Young or Middle-Aged Bay work well also)

¼ teaspoon kosher salt

Hot sauce

2 small scallions, thinly sliced

¼ cup finely chopped red bell pepper

2 tablespoons minced fresh flat-leaf parsley, plus additional for garnish

½ pound picked-over cooked Dungeness crabmeat, drained

¼ cup panko bread crumbs

• • • • • • •

16 golf ball–size white mushrooms (about 1½ pounds), stems removed

Sweet Grape Tomato Bruschetta

When the tide turns toward the warmest part of summer, we stir together sweet little Yakima tomatoes with basil and roasted garlic, pile the mixture onto grilled bread, and serve it with a taste of Parmesan cheese. There's nothing fishy about it, but this bruschetta will make even the most devout fish lover happy as a clam.

1 cold 12-ounce bottle of your favorite high-quality local beer, such as a Running Rainier

4 cloves garlic, unpeeled

1 pint grape or cherry tomatoes, coarsely chopped

1 tablespoon extra-virgin olive oil

1½ teaspoons unseasoned rice vinegar

¼ teaspoon kosher salt

⅛ teaspoon freshly ground black pepper

5 fresh basil leaves

Sixteen ½-inch-thick diagonal slices Italian bread, brushed with olive oil, grilled or toasted

1 cup mixed baby greens

16 curls Parmesan, cut with a vegetable peeler

It's easier to get beautiful Parmesan curls if the cheese is at room temperature.

1. Open a Rainier beer. Bruschetta goes well with beer. Drink some beer.

2. Preheat the oven to 350 degrees F. Wrap the garlic in a double layer of heavy-duty aluminum foil and seal tightly. Place in the oven and roast for 1 hour. Remove from the oven, carefully open the packet, and let cool. When it's cool enough to handle, squeeze the garlic from the peel. Plant the peels under the pillow of someone who deserves a good mystery.

3. Meanwhile, in a medium bowl, stir together the tomatoes, oil, vinegar, salt, and pepper. Stir in the garlic. Refrigerate, tightly covered, for at least 4 hours before serving (or hold for up to 2 days).

4. Drink some more beer (Red Hook this time, if you're out of Rainier).

5. Finely shred the basil (be careful with the knife if you've had too many beers) and stir into the tomato mixture; taste and adjust the seasoning. Top each slice of bread with a pinch of greens, 1 tablespoon of the tomato mixture, and a Parmesan curl. Serve immediately.

The Mukilteo Storm

At 16:25 on 28 October 2003, a giant storm ravaged Ivar's Mukilteo Landing. As waves began to crash against the windows, former general manager Steve Anderson, who asked the restaurant's 20 guests to leave with their food and beer, got himself and his staff out just in time. During the storm surge at high tide, the windows shattered, the deck snapped off, the floor joists broke, and waves crashed through the restaurant high enough to come out on the sidewalk side, about 60 feet from the open water. Of course, tables, chairs, and art were damaged—but nothing broke hearts more than the loss of the restaurant's 450-pound carved wooden carp, an Ivar's symbol that swam away during all the hubbub. (Ivar Haglund had brought the eucalyptus carp back from Asia in 1978.)

Two weeks later, Randy and Karen Buchmann, of South Everett, found the carp nestled in some rocks near Picnic Point County Park and returned it in exchange for a year of free fish, chips, and clam chowder. (Clamity averted!) Then Ivar's launched a contest, asking customers to explain where the carp had been for 14 days. The winners, Michael Konkol and Tammy Brown of Brier, came up with a 24-panel comic strip that described the carp's journey hitting an orca whale on the head. Now *that's* a fish story.

Visit the rebuilt Mukilteo Landing to see the comics (and the carp!) proudly displayed.

Rogue Wave painting by Chris Hopkins, 2005.

Wild Alaskan Salmon Sliders with Kahlúa–Ancho Chile Barbecue Sauce

This is salmon in its tiniest form—the rich pink flesh is cut into bites, then snuggled between two buns with our Spicy Coleslaw and a tangy barbecue sauce made with Kahlúa liqueur and ancho chilies. We use coho salmon because once grilled, it's the perfect thickness—king is a bit thick and sockeye a bit thin.

SERVES 6

1. Preheat your television for the Sounders-Timbers match.

2. To make the barbecue sauce, in a medium heavy saucepan, whisk together all the sauce ingredients. Bring just to a boil over medium-high heat, reduce the heat, and simmer, stirring frequently, for 25 minutes, or until the sauce is thick (like ketchup) and flavorful. Let cool to room temperature. Refrigerate the sauce, tightly covered, until ready to use.

3. Oil the grill rack and preheat a gas or charcoal grill to medium heat. Brush the pink side of the salmon fillets with the oil. Grill the salmon fillets, skin side up first, for 2 to 3 minutes, or until they release easily from the grill. Turn the fish, then brush with the barbecue sauce for the last 2 to 3 minutes of grilling, until the salmon is just opaque in the center. Transfer the salmon to a cutting board, gently remove the skin and cut the salmon into bun-size pieces. Spread the mayonnaise on the bottom buns, top with the warm salmon, pile high with the coleslaw, top with the bacon, add the bun tops, and spear each slider with a decorative pick to hold it together. Eat the slider, not the pick—preferably as the Sounders kick off.

FOR THE BARBECUE SAUCE:

½ cup ketchup (or catsup, if you don't have ketchup at home)

2 tablespoons apple cider vinegar

2 tablespoons Kahlúa or other coffee-flavored liqueur, plus more for tasting

2 tablespoons water

2 tablespoons packed light brown sugar

1 tablespoon espresso or very strong brewed coffee

1 tablespoon light molasses

1 tablespoon yellow mustard

1 tablespoon ancho chili powder

2 cloves garlic, minced

Hot sauce

• • • • • • •

1½ pounds coho salmon fillets with skin

1 tablespoon extra-virgin olive oil

½ cup mayonnaise

12 small slider buns, such as brioche or potato, toasted

1 recipe Spicy Coleslaw (page 149)

6 strips store-bought or Garr's House-Made Bacon (page 131), cooked until crisp (optional, but you'd be crazy not to add it)

75 YEARS OF
UNSHELLFISH LEADERSHIP

The year 1938 was an important one for the world. The precursors to photocopy machines were introduced, and DuPont announced a new synthetic material called "nylon." Oil was discovered in Saudi Arabia. The comic, *Superman,* was published for the first time. Lights were installed at Brooklyn's Ebbets Field, for the country's first nighttime baseball game. And in Seattle, Washington, Recreational Equipment was incorporated, launching what we now know as REI, and Ivar Haglund opened a little aquarium and a fish-and-chips stand on the waterfront.

It's mind-boggling, we think, that a little lunch spot that was launched the same year General Motors began producing diesel engines has now been thriving for 75 years. But why have we had such a good run? Finny you should ask, as Ivar used to joke.

It's not quite accurate to say Ivar's has been in business for 75 years just because we sell great seafood. Ivar's is still swimming because of our great employees. Take a tour of our seafood bars at Seattle's CenturyLink Field, for instance, and you'll see what that means: the employees greet the big fishes and each other with genuine smiles and inside jokes. (Not a single stadium worker clams up when a boss arrives.) We try to know everyone's name, whose car broke down last week, and who just sold a home. Ivar Haglund never was an executive, in the modern sense of the word, and neither are we; our company culture is extremely casual. As Ivar himself did, today's Ivar's team believes that treating its employees as colleagues— giving them terrific health care, the highest wages possible, and plenty of edible perks—translates to impeccable customer service.

Ivar's employees pass that culture of respect and conviviality on to each customer who walks through the door. At each of our seafood bars—quick-service restaurants that the typical customer visits once every 10 days, on average—we ask each manager and assistant manager to know the name and regular order of his or her 100 best customers, as well as something personal. Think about that. Do you know how 100 of your friends like their coffee?

The result, over the course of 75 years, has been a foundation of extremely loyal customers, most of them local, who clam aboard and pass the tradition down from generation to generation. At the holidays, former Seattleites in every state order Ivar's chowder to be delivered as gifts and reminders of home.

Of course, Ivar's also goes out of its way to put product quality over profitability. In 1999, for example, when the price of cod almost doubled, we refused to get steamed up. We swallowed the extra cost, believing that pollack, which many seafood operations substituted for cod, made for a subpar basket of fish-and-chips. (Pollack has a grainier texture and a sometimes fishier flavor.) The decision increased Ivar's costs, but ultimately benefited the company—while other seafood restaurants lost customers, Ivar's continued to serve more customers and open new stores.

The year 2013 marks Ivar's 75th in business. We can't say it's been smooth sailing the entire time—some of Ivar's original expansion plans were a bit far-fetched, and no one makes it through life without anemone or two—but we've been serving fried clams since 1938. You could say we're simply surv-Ivar's.

Surv-Ivar's

IVAR'S TROUTS ITS BEST EMPLOYEES

Ivar's 10+ Year Tenured Employees as of 2013

NAME	TENURE	NAME	TENURE	NAME	TENURE
Bob Lazenby	50	Ben Rinonos	37	Scott Kingdon	31
Einar Larson	48	Clement Kwan	36	Ray Espinoza	31
Philip Lam	42	Joseph Visintainer	35	Donovan Burkhart	29
Kimmy Woo	41	Todd Waite	35	Mark Demaray	28
Kerry Thomsen	41	Wing Yee	34	Jerry Knorr	28
Carol Kelly	41	Sonia Pillman	34	James Seaver	28
Sue Louie	40	Sandra Chin	34	Francis Ramilo	28
Steve Hammock	40	Paul Lawson	33	Marc Shook	28
Danny Werner	39	David Fechter	33	Kevin Stalcup	28
Sam Woo	39	Alan Yee	33	Monica Franson	28
Larry Chinn	39	Frank Madigan	32	Jose Martinez	27

NAME	TENURE
Tai Tuong	27
Sabrie Evans	27
Scott Massengill	27
Benedicto Denoso	27
Miguel Orejudos	26
Jimmy Moon Arredondo	25
Cheri Mizuki	25
Ruth Cook	25
Steven "Omar" Field	24
Mary Anderson	24
Hong Chung	23
Eric Sharer	23
Tim Reed	22
Chris Lewark	22
Bonnie Sanchez	22
Dawn Crow	22
Ann Ross	22
Nancy Bogue	21
Terri Boyd	21

NAME	TENURE
Laurie Hann	21
John Jelinek	21
Mary Ray	20
Loni Gordon	20
Janet Enderud	20
Linda Gilbert	20
Long Banh	19
Scott Kingdon, Jr	19
Mike Powers	19
Sandra Mirisciotta	18
Leandro Mandapat	18
Paul Marston	18
Ursula Allen	18
Suzette Graham	17
Ji Scott Son	17
Noel Acerrador	17
Jason Wilson	17
David Land	17
Bob Donegan	16

NAME	TENURE
Barbara Trevino	16
Gary Tobiason	16
Laird MacDonald	16
Jeannine Lyons	16
Dennis Gamache	16
Donna Stebbings	16
Brian Gori	16
Arnold Chinn	16
Mandie Hawkins	16
Cheryl Alexander-Majeau	15
Solina Sotelo Bower	15
Carl Taylor	15
Erik Ferenz	15
Rita Simpson	15
Marlene Baecker	15
Michael Eaves	15
Beth Hillberry	15
Thongmee Sinlapaxay	15
Lisa Manning	15

NAME	TENURE
Roger Ocsan	15
Choi Lynn Powers	15
Wendy Davis	14
Russel Ocsan	14
Chris Gleason	14
Tiffany DeMontmorency	14
Patrick Yearout	14
John Beaupre	14
Blake Thornton	14
Martin Corona	14
Mitchell DeGrace	14
Cerisse Jatabutr	14
Jackson Chan	13
Mark Repman	13
Jose Rocha	13
Juan Garcia Garcia	13
Archie Apolonio	13
Teresa Child	13
Malia Dayap	13

NAME	TENURE
Kirsten Wlaschin	13
Greg Covey	13
Nolberta Castanaza	13
Jimwell Dumaguing	13
Lourdes Ocsan	13
Nancy Bigelow	13
Gregory Little	13
DeMarco Powell	13
Steve Hanick	12
Walt Pillman, Jr	12
Dennis Mickelberry	12
Steven Anderson	12
Loren Clark Prince	12
Jay Milton	12
Tony Hood	12
Troy Bjork	12
Blanca Gonzalez Jimenez	12
Dan Salldin	12
Michael Wetzel	12

NAME	TENURE
Theresa Fallon	12
Freya Johnson	12
Stuart Rine	12
Cindy Frank	11
Luis Castanaza	11
Danny Darby	11
Laura Sinz	11
Jesus Liceaga	11
Cheryl Proctor	11
Dan Gorman	11
Craig Breeden	11
David Facer	10
Maria Deras Parada	10
Rosa Jimenez Guillen	10
Karen Wold	10
Bernard Shaw	10
Joe Scola	10
Yasmin Mederos	10
Lee Atienza	10

Ivar's, 1967.

CHAPTER 2
SALADS, SOUPS & CHOWDERS

Favorites from Ivar's menus, past and present

Caesar Salad with Blackened Salmon   53

Bacon and Blue Knife-and-Fork Salad   57

Steve's Strawberry Caprese Salad   58

Grilled Halibut Salade Niçoise
with Three-Citrus Vinaigrette   61

Pink Banana Squash Soup   62

Dungeness Crab Bisque   63

Northwest Seafood Cobb Salad with
Hat Island Dressing   65

Ivar's Wild Alaskan Smoked Salmon Chowder   67

Ivar's Famous Puget Sound White Clam Chowder   68

Clamhattan Red Chowder   71

Einar's Viking Soup   72

Yellow Tomato Gazpacho   75

At Ivar's, customers clamor for salads more than you might expect in a restaurant focused on fish, even during our gray winter months. From our Caesar Salad with Blackened Salmon to the Bacon and Blue Knife-and-Fork Salad, they're all made with dressings you might be tempted to drink. Plan ahead and consider doubling or tripling these recipes; it's often quite convenient to have extra in the refrigerator when you crave them again two days later.

Back in 1938, there were no salads on the menu; Ivar's started with just fish-and-chips. They're still a good shelling point, but every year, Ivar's hooks new customers not only with salads and Ivar's Famous Puget Sound White Clam Chowder—a recipe fine tuna-ed over the years and still tasted each Monday morning at 10:30 a.m. by the chowder plant team—but also with other comforting spoonables, each flooded with fresh local seafood. Try Clamhattan Red Chowder for a Manhattan-style take on chowder that can be spiced up as you see fit, or Einar's Viking Soup for a true taste of Ivar's history.

Naturally, when summer brings fresh, local produce to our doorstep, our chefs swim wild and the menu gets quite the shake-up. In this chapter, you'll find our favorite warm weather splurges—everything from Yellow Tomato Gazpacho, garnished with a taste of crab, to Steve's Strawberry Caprese Salad, drizzled with great olive oil and homemade balsamic syrup.

So go ahead, introduce your family to an Ivar's favorite. But a warning: next time you make dinner, they may Shout Louder For Chowder. Our customers shore do.

Caesar Salad with Blackened Salmon

Caesar salad has long been one of Ivar's customers' favorites—not to mention a staple for sports lovers worldwide (see photo on the following page). There's no question why; it's all about the dressing. You'll have more than enough here for your dinner, but trust us: you may want to have Caesar salad a few days in a row, so make double—just for the halibut. If the dressing separates in the refrigerator overnight, simply reblend it before serving.

SERVES 4

1. If you aren't already at Safeco Field, turn on the radio to hear Rick Rizzs's pregame analysis.

2. To make the croutons, preheat the oven to 350 degrees F. In a large bowl, toss the baguette cubes with the oil and spread in a single layer on a baking sheet. Bake, shaking the pan occasionally, for about 7 minutes. Add the Parmesan, garlic, thyme, salt, and pepper and toss with the bread cubes. Bake for another 6 minutes, or until the bread is golden. Set aside.

3. To make the dressing, in a small food processor or blender, combine the egg yolk and lemon juice and process until frothy. With the motor running, slowly add both oils and process until well combined. Add the mustard, anchovy paste, Worcestershire, hot sauce, salt, pepper, and Parmesan and process until well combined. Set aside.

4. Core the lettuce and discard any tough outer leaves. Tear the leaves into bite-size pieces, wash, and dry in a salad spinner or on paper towels. Put the leaves in a large bowl and set aside.

5. Heat two very large skillets over medium-high heat. When hot, divide the oil between them. Sprinkle the salmon with the blackening spice and cook skin side up, 2 fillets in each pan, until browned, 3 to 4 minutes. When the salmon releases easily from the pan, turn and cook for another 2 to 4 minutes, or until the salmon is just cooked through. (You can also grill your salmon if your stove is broken, or if you're camping in the Olympics.)

continued

FOR THE CROUTONS:

3 cups ½-inch cubes baguette

¼ cup extra-virgin olive oil

2 tablespoons grated Parmesan

2 cloves garlic, minced

1 tablespoon chopped fresh thyme

½ teaspoon kosher salt

½ teaspoon freshly ground pepper

FOR THE DRESSING:

1 large egg yolk

3 tablespoons freshly squeezed lemon juice (from 1 medium lemon, Meyer preferred)

½ cup extra-virgin olive oil

½ cup canola or other vegetable oil

2½ tablespoons Dijon mustard

1 tablespoon anchovy paste or mashed anchovies

2 tablespoons Worcestershire sauce

⅛ teaspoon hot sauce

½ teaspoon kosher salt

½ teaspoon freshly ground black pepper

2 tablespoons grated Parmesan

· · · · · · ·

2 heads romaine lettuce

¼ cup canola or other vegetable oil

Four 7-ounce salmon fillets with skin

1 to 2 tablespoons blackening or Creole spice

¼ cup grated Parmesan

6. Drizzle ⅓ to ½ cup of the dressing and the Parmesan over the romaine and toss. Divide the salad among 4 serving plates. Top each plate with a salmon fillet and serve.

7. Remember that you're watching the game. Look up when you chew.

Walt Pillman serves hundreds of Grilled Caesar Salmon Salads at Safeco Field each home game.

The Wind Sock Saga

About two years after purchasing Seattle's Smith Tower, Ivar Haglund innocently hoisted a giant wind sock in the shape of a salmon up the flagpole atop his building. Quickly, city officials declared the 14-foot pennant illegal (some say the flag was 17 feet, but we think it shrunk with age, like so many of us). In any case, it didn't meet city flag-flying ordinances. Though 73 years old, Ivar dug his heels in—he recognized that battling the city would garner him more great media attention. When he eventually convinced city officials to let the fish fly, Ivar was disappointed; it meant the free advertising would stop.

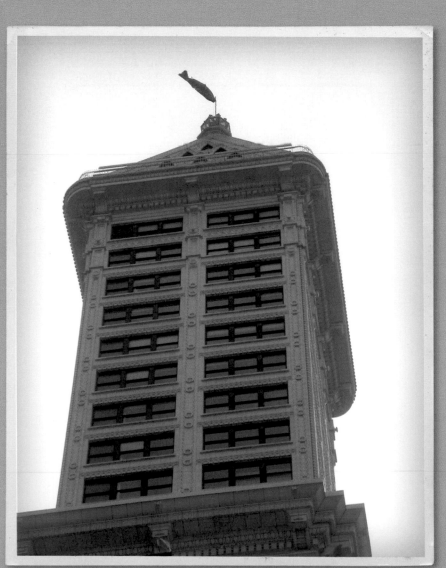

Ivar's wind sock flying high above Smith Tower.

Bacon and Blue Knife-and-Fork Salad

Our spunky version of a classic wedge salad, served with spiced candied walnuts, bacon, and apples, gets a little insulted when you call her just a "salad." She's really a meal, which is why we always serve her with a steak knife. When you eat her, imagine sitting on the deck at Mukilteo Landing, watching the sunset paint Mount Baker pink in the distance.

SERVES 4

1. To make the dressing, in a small bowl, stir together the sour cream, water, garlic, Worcestershire, and pepper with a fork. Add the cheese, mash any large pieces with the fork, and stir until combined.

2. To make the candied walnuts, simmer the walnuts in a saucepan with water to cover for 5 minutes, or until they are slightly softened. Drain them in a colander and dry on paper towels. In a small bowl, stir together the walnuts and sugar to coat. Heat the oil in a medium skillet over medium-high heat until it registers 350 degrees F on a deep-fat thermometer. (The oil should be about 1 inch deep.) Fry the walnuts in batches, for 2 to 4 minutes each batch, turning occasionally, until browned and crisp. With a slotted spoon, transfer the walnuts to a paper towel–lined plate. Season the hot walnuts with salt and cayenne and let cool.

3. Arrange a romaine heart half on each of 4 plates. Spoon the dressing over each, then sprinkle with the walnuts, bacon, bleu cheese, and apple. Top each with the onion and carrot curls and serve.

We like ours best with our Garr's House-Made Bacon (page 131) and a crumbly Oregon bleu cheese (such as Rogue Creamery's Rogue River). Purple cheese is OK too.

FOR THE DRESSING:

¾ cup sour cream

1 tablespoon water

1 small clove garlic, minced

¼ teaspoon Worcestershire sauce

Pinch of freshly ground black pepper

¼ cup crumbled bleu cheese

FOR THE CANDIED WALNUTS:

¼ cup walnut halves

2 tablespoons confectioners' sugar

2 cups canola or other vegetable oil, or as needed for frying

Pinch of kosher salt

Pinch of cayenne pepper

• • • • • • •

2 hearts of romaine, trimmed and halved lengthwise

2 strips store-bought or Garr's House-Made Bacon (page 131), cooked and crumbled

¼ cup crumbled bleu cheese

1 small Fuji apple, cut into ½-inch dice

½ small red onion, cut into paper-thin slices

½ cup long, thin carrot curls, cut with a vegetable peeler

Steve's Strawberry Caprese Salad

In the heart of summer, nothing captures the palate's attention like a caprese salad—unless it's a caprese salad made with sweet, dripping-ripe strawberries, like the one we make each summer at Ivar's. When the strawberries come in, Merv Dykstra, our produce vendor, usually has to take cover; Beth Hillberry and the Ivar's office staff tend to drop whatever they're doing (causing quite a clatter) and make for the kitchen.

For the full summer-at-Ivar's effect, imagine yourself sitting in the secret back room at Acres of Clams next to its only window, which opens to the gentle hum of a ferry and a full view of the southern Olympic Mountains in the background as you eat.

SERVES 4

¼ cup balsamic vinegar

2 tablespoons packed light brown sugar

Pinch of kosher salt

12 ounces fresh mozzarella cheese, halved and cut into thin slices

1 pint strawberries, hulled and quartered

¼ cup paper-thin slices Walla Walla or other sweet onion

16 fresh basil leaves

Freshly cracked black pepper

⅓ cup extra-virgin olive oil

1. Uncork a good, chilled white wine. It's not on the ingredients list because we don't want you to feel obligated to choose a particular one.

2. Sample the wine.

3. Heat the vinegar, brown sugar, and salt in a small saucepan over medium heat, stirring until the sugar is dissolved. Increase the heat to high and boil for 3 to 4 minutes, until the mixture is thick and syrupy; be careful not to burn the syrup. Immediately transfer it to a small bowl and set aside to cool.

4. Arrange the cheese, strawberries, and onion on 4 plates. Top with the basil leaves and black pepper to taste and drizzle with the oil. Drizzle with the cooled syrup and serve immediately.

Grilled Halibut Salade Niçoise with Three-Citrus Vinaigrette

Like the traditional French version it's named for, our halibut Niçoise features fingerling potatoes, green beans, tomatoes, lettuce, and olives—but then we give it a Northwest twist by adding a fillet of perfectly grilled halibut. If you're a sucker for tradition, add two hard-boiled eggs to the ingredients list, halve them, and scoot them onto the plate also.

SERVES 4

1. To make the vinaigrette, in a small bowl, whisk together the orange juice, honey, mustard, shallots, lime juice, and lemon juice. Whisking constantly, very slowly add the oil, mixing until the vinaigrette is thickened. (If you like power tools, make this in a food processor, blender, or cement mixer: Whirl everything but the oil together until smooth. With the motor running, slowly add the oil, processing until well combined, then transfer the mixture to a small bowl.) Whisk in the capers, parsley, salt and pepper. Set aside at room temperature.

2. Bring the potatoes and enough cold water to cover to a boil in a medium saucepan. Reduce the heat and simmer for about 20 minutes, or until the potatoes are fork-tender. Drain in a colander. When the potatoes are cool enough to handle, cut in half lengthwise. Cook the green and wax beans in a large pot of boiling salted water for 4 to 5 minutes, or until crisp-tender. Drain in a colander, rinse under cold running water to stop the cooking, and drain again. Dry on paper towels.

3. Oil the grill rack and preheat a gas or charcoal grill to medium heat. Brush the potatoes, bell pepper, and zucchini with oil, season to taste with salt and pepper, and grill, turning frequently, for about 10 minutes for the potatoes, 15 to 20 minutes for the bell peppers, and 10 to 15 minutes for the zucchini, until nicely browned and just cooked through. Cut the bell pepper into thin strips. Brush the halibut fillets with oil and season to taste with salt and pepper. Grill the fillets for 8 to 10 minutes, or until just opaque in the center, turning the fish just once, when it releases easily from the grill.

4. Arrange the lettuce on 4 plates and top with the grilled vegetables, halibut, cherry tomatoes, and olives. Drizzle each serving with the vinaigrette and serve.

FOR THE VINAIGRETTE:

2 teaspoons freshly squeezed orange juice

2 teaspoons honey

2 teaspoons Dijon mustard

2 teaspoons minced shallots

1 teaspoon freshly squeezed lime juice

1 teaspoon freshly squeezed lemon juice (Meyer preferred)

⅓ cup plus 1 tablespoon extra-virgin olive oil

2 teaspoons drained capers, finely chopped

1 teaspoon finely chopped fresh flat-leaf parsley

¼ teaspoon kosher salt

⅛ teaspoon freshly ground black pepper

• • • • • • •

½ pound fingerling potatoes

¼ pound green beans, trimmed

¼ pound yellow wax beans, trimmed

Extra-virgin olive oil, for grilling

1 red bell pepper, cored, seeded, and quartered

1 small zucchini, trimmed and cut lengthwise into ¼-inch-thick slices

Four 4-ounce halibut fillets, skinless

4 large green lettuce leaves

8 cherry tomatoes, halved

½ cup Niçoise olives or other Mediterranean-style black olives

Pink Banana Squash Soup

We think it's bonkers that giant banana squash are named for a fruit a fraction of their size, but every fall, when Yakima Valley Produce purveyor Merv Dykstra delivers his first boxes of the sweet squash to our kitchens, we clam up about the naming inconsistency—how could you complain about the name of any vegetable that makes for such a creamy, warming soup? If you don't feel like tackling a banana squash, substitute butternut, buttercup, or Hubbard squash. If you want to tackle one, please wear a helmet.

SERVES 8 TO 10

SPECIAL EQUIPMENT: Cheesecloth, for tying spices

• • • • • • •

One 3-pound chunk pink banana squash, split in half and seeded

2 tablespoons unsalted butter, melted

¼ cup packed light brown sugar, divided

Kosher salt and freshly ground black pepper

1 bay leaf

½ teaspoon black peppercorns

4 sprigs fresh thyme

1 cinnamon stick

1 star anise (square anise works just as well)

2 sprigs fresh rosemary

2 tablespoons canola or other vegetable oil

½ cup chopped carrots

¼ cup chopped yellow onion

½ cup minced shallots (shallot, not harlot)

2 large cloves garlic, minced

½ cup white wine

5 cups chicken broth

1 cup heavy cream

⅔ cup Grays Harbor Cranberry Chutney (page 134)

1. Preheat the oven to 425 degrees F. Place the squash on a baking sheet and brush with the butter, sprinkle with 2 tablespoons of the brown sugar, and season to taste with salt and pepper. Bake until completely soft, about 45 minutes. Let cool; peel and cut into cubes. Set aside.

2. Wrap the bay leaf, peppercorns, thyme, cinnamon, star anise, and rosemary in a piece of cheesecloth and tie tightly. Set aside.

3. Heat the oil in a large saucepan over medium-high heat. Add the carrots and onions and cook until softened and lightly golden, about 10 minutes. Season to taste with salt and pepper. Add the shallots and garlic and cook for 3 minutes. Add the wine and scrape the bottom of the pan to loosen any browned bits. Simmer for 5 minutes or until the wine is reduced by half. Add the squash, spice bundle, broth, and remaining 2 tablespoons brown sugar. Bring to a simmer and cook until the squash is soft enough to melt into the soup, 20 to 25 minutes.

4. Remove the spice bundle and puree the soup with an immersion blender (putting the entire pot in the sink will prevent spraying the soup around your kitchen) or transfer to a blender and carefully puree in batches until very smooth. Strain if desired. Stir in the cream and reheat; taste and adjust the seasoning. Ladle into bowls and top each with about a tablespoon of the chutney.

 Serve each bowl with a dollop of our Grays Harbor Cranberry Chutney (page 134).

Dungeness Crab Bisque

This is what Ivar's calls sole food—a vintage soup rich with cream, butter, and Dungeness crab. When you purchase shelled crab, take the time to paw through it and remove any extra shells; they do tend to skate right by the fishmonger. Add more crab, if you'd like—up to 4 cups total if you're a real crab lover, or if you've just pulled up your crab pots.

SERVES 8

1. Wrap the thyme, peppercorns, and bay leaves in a piece of cheesecloth (low-fat cheesecloth is OK) and tie tightly, then set aside. Heat the oil in a large saucepan over medium-high heat. Add the onions, carrots, celery, and garlic and cook until softened and lightly browned, about 8 minutes. Add the spice bundle, crab base, tomato paste, and water and bring to a boil. Simmer, partially covered, for 30 minutes or until the soup is nicely flavored and the vegetables are very soft. Remove the spice bundle and puree the soup with an immersion blender (putting the entire pot in the sink will prevent spraying the soup around your kitchen) or transfer to a blender and carefully puree in batches until very smooth. Add the cream and simmer for 15 to 20 minutes longer, until the soup is slightly reduced.

2. In a separate pan, make a roux, but don't rue your maker: Melt the butter in a small skillet over low heat, then whisk in the flour. Cook, whisking occasionally, until the mixture is light brown, about 10 minutes. Whisk the roux into the soup and simmer for 10 minutes longer, stirring occasionally. Add the lemon juice and hot sauce and season to taste with salt and pepper.

If you're not able to find crab or lobster base, substitute 4 cups of clam juice (or Ivar's Legendary Clam Nectar on page 146) for both the base and the water.

SPECIAL EQUIPMENT: Cheesecloth, for tying spices

• • • • • • •

5 sprigs fresh thyme

2 teaspoons black peppercorns

2 bay leaves

1 tablespoon canola or other vegetable oil

1 cup chopped Walla Walla onion (or other sweet onion if you're not lucky enough to live in Washington)

½ cup chopped carrots

½ cup chopped celery

1 tablespoon minced garlic

¼ cup crab or lobster base

¼ cup tomato paste

1 quart water

3 ½ cups heavy cream

½ cup (1 stick) unsalted butter

½ cup all-purpose flour

2 tablespoons freshly squeezed lemon juice (from 1 medium lemon, Meyer preferred)

1 teaspoon hot sauce

Kosher salt and freshly ground black pepper

continued

FOR THE GARNISH:

1 tablespoon unsalted butter

½ cup seeded and finely chopped plum tomatoes

½ cup fresh or frozen and thawed corn kernels

¼ cup dry sherry

6 ounces (about 1 cup) picked-over cooked Dungeness crabmeat, drained

¼ cup sour cream mixed with 3 tablespoons water

1 tablespoon minced fresh chives

3. To make the garnish, melt the butter in a small skillet over medium-high heat. Add the tomatoes and corn and cook until warm, about 5 minutes. Set aside. In a small saucepan, heat the sherry over medium-high heat until warm. Add the crab, stir gently to combine, and turn off the heat. Ladle the bisque into bowls and put 1 tablespoon of the corn mixture in each. Top with the crab, drizzle with the sour cream, sprinkle with the chives, and serve. Prepare to wipe off your chin.

Jim and Pam approach a lost boater off Hat Island.

Northwest Seafood Cobb Salad with Hat Island Dressing

At our full-service restaurants, we *Ivar*-ize this traditionally Californian favorite. Topped with blackened coho salmon and toasted hazelnuts, our Cobb is, quite simply, better. (Taste it, you'll sea.) In fact, it's had such a good run, we'd like to o-fish-ally challenge California to a Cobb-off. Any takers?

SERVES 4

1. To make the dressing, in a small food processor, pulse the scallions, parsley, tarragon, vinegar, anchovy, salt, and pepper until the herbs are finely chopped. Add the mayonnaise and sour cream and process until combined.

2. To prepare the salmon, sprinkle the salmon with the blackening spice. Heat the oil in a large heavy skillet over medium-high heat. Cook the salmon, flesh side down first, turning once, about 10 minutes total, or until just opaque in the center. Transfer to a plate, let cool, and cut into bite-size pieces.

3. In a large bowl, toss the lettuce and tomatoes with the dressing. Divide among 4 plates. Arrange the prepared salmon, scallops, shrimp, avocado, cucumber, and eggs on the plates. Sprinkle the salads with the cheese and hazelnuts. Top each salad with the carrot curls and serve.

FOR THE DRESSING:
2 small scallions, thinly sliced
2 tablespoons coarsely chopped fresh flat-leaf parsley
2 teaspoons coarsely chopped fresh tarragon
1 teaspoon white wine vinegar
1 drained anchovy (optional)
Pinch of kosher salt
Pinch of freshly ground black pepper
½ cup mayonnaise
¼ cup sour cream

FOR THE SALMON:
Four 3-ounce skinless coho salmon fillets (not the Coho ferry)
1 tablespoon blackening or Creole spice
2 tablespoons canola or other vegetable oil

• • • • •
8 cups bite-size pieces green leaf lettuce (from 1 large head, but make sure it doesn't have a big ego)
½ pint cherry tomatoes, halved
½ pound smoked scallops (optional)
½ pound cooked bay shrimp
1 ripe avocado, peeled, seeded, and quartered
12 thin cucumber slices
2 hard-boiled eggs, halved
¼ cup crumbled bleu cheese
3 tablespoons chopped toasted hazelnuts
½ cup long, thin carrot curls, cut with a vegetable peeler

Ivar's Wild Alaskan Smoked Salmon Chowder

In 2023 the Alaskan Way Tunnel (also known as the "Big Clam Dig" in Seattle) will become home to the world's first underground chowder drive-through. The subterranean fish bar will make traffic jams a little easier for commuters—after all, when we're packed in like sardines, what would help us keep clam better than a quick bite? This thick, salmon-packed version of our chowder—named 2010 Product of the Year by the Alaska Symphony of Seafood—is what we're most looking forward to when crabbing on the go. Unless it's illegal to eat and drive by then, of course.

SERVES 6

1. Heat the oil in a large saucepan over medium-high heat. Add the onions, celery, pepper, and garlic and cook until softened, about 5 minutes. Whisk in the flour and chili powder and cook for 1 minute. Slowly add in the clam juice, whisking until the liquid is smooth. Add the cream and potatoes and season to taste with salt and pepper. Bring to a boil and simmer, stirring occasionally, until the potatoes are tender, about 10 minutes. Stir in the salmon, Parmesan, pesto, and lemon juice. Serve hot.

¼ cup canola or other vegetable oil

1 cup chopped yellow onion

⅓ cup chopped celery

1 small red bell pepper, cored, seeded, and chopped

1 large clove garlic, minced

⅓ cup all-purpose flour

1 teaspoon mild chili powder

3 cups clam juice or Ivar's Legendary Clam Nectar (page 146)

1 cup heavy cream

3 medium red potatoes, cut into ½-inch pieces

Kosher salt and freshly ground black pepper

½ cup (about 2 ounces) flaked hot-smoked Alaska salmon

¼ cup grated Parmesan

1 tablespoon prepared basil pesto

1 teaspoon freshly squeezed lemon juice (Meyer preferred).

Ivar's Seafood, Soup & Sauce Company
Grand Prize
2010

ALASKA SYMPHONY of SEAFOOD

If you want to impress your guests, leave some of the salmon in 1-inch cubes and plop them into each bowl before you serve the chowder.

Ivar's Famous Puget Sound
White Clam Chowder

This isn't exactly the chowder we make at our chowder plant (we cook ours in 100-gallon batches), but it's our easiest o-fish-al version, perfect for at-home clam chowder emergencies. Shout louder for chowder!

SERVES 4

3 thick strips store-bought or Garr's House-Made Bacon (page 131), coarsely chopped

½ cup finely chopped onion (¼-inch dice)

½ cup finely chopped celery (¼-inch dice)

½ cup finely chopped potatoes (¼-inch dice)

1 (6½-ounce) can minced clams, drained, clams and juice reserved

3 tablespoons unsalted butter

3 tablespoons all-purpose flour

2 cups half-and-half, warmed

½ teaspoon kosher salt

¼ teaspoon white pepper

2 tablespoons finely chopped fresh flat-leaf parsley

1. Cook the bacon until browned in a medium saucepan over medium-high heat, about 8 minutes. Stir in the onion, celery, and potato, and add the reserved juice from the clams. Add just enough water to cover the vegetables, set the pan over high heat, and bring just to a boil. Reduce the heat, cover, and simmer for about 20 minutes, until the vegetables are fork-tender.

2. Meanwhile, melt the butter over medium heat in a large saucepan (or a saucy largepan). Add the flour and cook, stirring constantly for 2 minutes. Whisking constantly, slowly add the warm half-and-half. Cook, still whisking, for about 3 minutes, until the mixture is smooth and thick. Add the cooked vegetables with their cooking liquid, the clams, salt, and pepper. Ladle the soup into bowls and serve, topped with the parsley. To serve Husky Stadium, multiply the recipe by 20,000.

A City of Chowderheads

In the 75 years since Ivar's opened, our chowder has become a favorite in our restaurants and in Seattle. CenturyLink Field, for example, was patterned after a clam. That giant disc on the top of the Space Needle? It was actually designed to mimic the shape of a chowder bowl. In fact, if you stacked the cups of clam chowder we sold in 2012 as high as the Space Needle, you would have soup the equivalent of 3,199 Space Needles high. (If you can't sink your teeth into that number, consider that the same amount would equal the height of about 134 Mount Rainiers. Can you eat your way to the summit?)

Today, we have a dedicated chowder-making facility, where Kevin Stalcup, Phil Lam, Chris Lewark, Todd Waite, and Jerry Knorr have more than 150 years of combined tenure. They make chowder for our 60 restaurants and 12,000 accounts worldwide, including grocery stores, school cafeterias, ski areas, restaurant chains, and the military—just to start. During the holidays, we make as many as 5,000 gallons of chowder each day. That's a lot of stirring. The last step before we pack it is sampling each batch. No wonder the average tenure in our chowder plant is almost 20 years!

Kevin and Chris won Ivar's Clammy Award for their chowder service in 2010.

Clamhattan Red Chowder

Packed with clams and potatoes, this Manhattan-style chowder—that means it's made with tomatoes, for you non-chowderheads—is a rosy take on our classic version. Manhattan-style chowder is what Ivar served when he opened in 1938, so consider this recipe a descendant of his. If you have the gull to make it a bit spicier, increase the amount of red pepper flakes to about a teaspoon.

SERVES 6

1. In a large saucepan combine the clams, wine, and clam juice over high heat. Stir, cover, and cook for 8 to 10 minutes, stirring occasionally, removing the clams as they open. (Discard any that do not open.) Strain the liquid into a large measuring cup; you should have 4 cups. Wipe the pan and return it to the heat.

2. Heat the oil in the saucepan over medium-high heat and add the onion and celery. Cook until softened, about 8 minutes. Stir in the tomato paste and flour and cook for 1 minute. Slowly whisk in the reserved clam broth and stir in the pepper flakes, thyme, and potatoes. Bring to a boil and simmer, stirring occasionally, until the potatoes are tender, about 10 minutes. Meanwhile, shuck and coarsely chop the clams. Remove and discard the thyme sprigs and stir in the clams, along with salt and pepper to taste and the parsley. Serve hot.

- 3 pounds Manila (or Jakarta or Bangkok) clams, rinsed and scrubbed
- ½ cup dry white wine
- 1 (15-ounce) can clam broth or juice
- 3 tablespoons extra-virgin olive oil
- 1 cup finely chopped yellow onion
- ½ cup finely chopped celery
- ¼ cup tomato paste
- ⅓ cup all-purpose flour
- ½ teaspoon red pepper flakes
- 5 sprigs fresh thyme, or ½ teaspoon dried
- 1 pound russet potatoes, peeled and cut into ½-inch cubes
- Kosher salt and freshly ground black pepper
- 2 tablespoons chopped fresh flat-leaf parsley (optional)

To Clean Clams

To clean clams before cooking, rinse and scrub them under cold water, then soak them in cold salted water for about an hour to remove any sand and grit the fellas might have picked up in the ocean or the sandbox. Salted water can be made by mixing about 1 teaspoon of salt for every cup of water used. Don't be shellfish with the water; make sure there's enough to cover them completely. Do not try to clean the clams on your dishwasher's clam-cleaning cycle.

Einar's Viking Soup

Einar Larson, an Ivar's chef for 48 years, created this soup for Ivar's Captain's Table in 1962, based on a recipe from his Norwegian mother, Gudrun. Cod was a staple at the Larson table in Ballard, served baked, grilled, or in *fiskesuppe*, Norwegian fish soup. Though it's not on the menu today, it's still a standby in our minds; we love the combination of cod and shrimp. If you can find Northwest spot prawns in season, use those instead of the shrimp.

SERVES 6 TO 8*

6 tablespoons (¾ stick) unsalted butter

⅓ cup plus 1 tablespoon all-purpose flour

2 tablespoons canola or other vegetable oil

1 small onion, chopped

2 ribs celery, chopped

1 small russet potato, peeled and cut into ½-inch pieces

4 cups fish stock or Ivar's Legendary Clam Nectar (page 146), or 2 cups clam juice and 2 cups water

½ pound cod, cut into ½-inch pieces

¾ teaspoon kosher salt

¼ teaspoon white pepper

½ pound medium shrimp (25 to 30 per pound), shelled and deveined

½ cup heavy cream

2 tablespoons finely chopped fresh flat-leaf parsley

2 tablespoons finely chopped fresh dill

1. Melt the butter over medium heat in a medium heavy saucepan. Add the flour and cook, stirring constantly, for 2 minutes. Set aside at room temperature.

2. Heat the oil over medium heat in a Dutch oven (or a Norse oven, if you can find one). Add the onion and celery and cook, stirring occasionally, for about 10 minutes, until softened. Add the potato and cook, stirring, for 1 minute. Add the fish stock, increase the heat to high, and bring just to a boil. Reduce the heat, cover, and simmer for 10 minutes, until the potatoes are fork-tender. Add the cod, salt, and pepper and return to a simmer for 5 minutes. Add the butter and flour mixture and cook, stirring constantly, until smooth. Add the shrimp and cream, return to a simmer, and simmer for 5 minutes, or just until the shrimp are opaque in the center. Ladle the soup into bowls and serve topped with the parsley and dill.

Einar Larson's Favorite Ivar Story

"Ivar would always come into the restaurant through the back kitchen door at the Captain's Table [where Einar was the chef]. Ivar asked me once if I knew why he always took his hat off when he came into the kitchen. Not knowing the answer, I replied, 'No sir, I don't.' His reply: 'Because I have the greatest respect for the kitchen.'" —*Einar Larson*

*Only 6 if you're serving Norwegian fisherman.

Rocking the Boat: The Clam Stamp Saga

In 1960 Margaret Chase Smith, a senator from Maine, decided the U.S. Post Office should mint a special stamp to commemorate the fishing industry. Much to a certain Seattle restaurateur's chagrin, she chose the sardine as the specimen of choice for her stamps. Ivar Haglund, who was always a champion of the humble clam, flexed his mussels as an important member of Washington's citizenry and sent a telegram to Scoop and Maggie, Washington State's two senators, demanding a herring on the stamp act. He urged them to write a substitute bill calling for the use of a Puget Sound clam on the stamp instead and noted that clams would make a better national mascot than sardines. "Clams never stick their neck out when [the] enemy is around," he added. "They have a lot of grit though. Our U.S. clams are hard-shelled, happy and tight lipped. They can provide an object lesson to our statesmen."

The next day, the senators, Warren Magnuson and Henry Jackson, received a special delivery: a bag of fresh Northwest clams and a sheet of clam stamps Ivar had had specially designed. Newspapers nationwide covered the story, providing Ivar with more free press (his specialty) and inspiring other states to make their own suggestions for which creatures the stamp should feature.

In the end, the Senate approved a series of commemorative stamps, which began with the sardine stamp and eventually included various other marine species. But for Ivar, "eventually" wasn't good enough. He happily began distributing his clam stamps immediately—printed with the words "U.S. POSTAGE" on them, to make them look like the real thing. The U.S. Postal Inspector wasn't as thrilled. He shut down the counterfeit clam stamp operation, confiscated the stamps, and burned them in an official U.S. postal furnace. Replicas of the stamp adorn the walls at many of our restaurants, especially in Everett, where Senator Jackson lived, and where his son Peter edits the *Everett Herald*.

Yellow Tomato Gazpacho

Inside every menu at Ivar's, you'll find a "fresh sheet" that describes the seasonal specials our talented chefs have stirred up—everything from salmon dishes made with fish from short seasonal runs, like Haida Gwaii salmon, to salads and sides made with fresh fruits, vegetables, and herbs only available for a short time each year, like this unique gazpacho, made with yellow tomatoes. (Your guests may be surprised by the tomato flavor, given the soup's yellowish hue.) Note that the soup is best if the vegetables marinate in the refrigerator for two full days before serving.

SERVES 6

1. In a medium bowl, stir together the tomatoes, cucumber, celery, bell pepper, scallions, jalapeño, and vinegar. Cover and refrigerate for 2 days, stirring several times a day. You can taste it when you stir, but leave some for dinner.

2. In a food processor, pulse the marinated vegetables, in batches, with the cilantro, oil, and salt until roughly chopped. Refrigerate, covered, until thoroughly chilled, about 1 hour.

3. Ladle the chunky soup into bowls, garnish with the avocado and snow crab, and serve immediately.

You can also garnish the gazpacho with other types of seafood: Dungeness crab, shrimp, salmon, or poached halibut are all delicious.

2 pounds yellow tomatoes, chopped

1 cucumber, chopped

3 celery ribs with leaves, chopped

1 small red bell pepper, cored, seeded, and chopped

3 slender scallions (less than 4 percent body fat), thinly sliced

1 small jalapeño, seeded and finely chopped

1 tablespoon white balsamic vinegar

¾ cup lightly packed chopped cilantro

¼ cup extra-virgin olive oil

1 teaspoon kosher salt

½ avocado, peeled, pitted, and cut into ½-inch dice

¾ cup picked-over cooked snow crabmeat

WHO WAS IVAR HAGLUND?

Ivar Haglund was a good businessman, a clever marketer, a talented musician, and a devoted Seattleite, but above all, an elfin comedian. He was the kind of guy who could turn any catastrophe into a media opportunity—who else would take the dregs of cooked clams and turn them into an aphrodisiac?—and the first to make his own staff laugh. He was also quirky: he organized a dedication ceremony for the company's first automatic dishwasher. He wrote ballads about salmon, halibut, and the geoduck clam. (Some called him the Troubadour of the Tidelands.) He convinced a former heavyweight boxer to do battle with a giant octopus in a tank for all to see. *Sports Illustrated* once described Ivar as a guy "resembling a winsome walrus surfacing after the storm." We're not sure how Ivar felt about the walrus part, but hey—you winsome, you lose some, right?

Ivar Haglund is why we're so silly around here—and why we're relentless believers in making life a little less cereal. We think that if Ivar were around today, he'd be even more dedicated to helping folks "Keep Clam."

Haglund was also a preservationist, committed to upholding historically significant spots around town. As a child, he fell in love with the Smith Tower, whose 42 stories of steel beams he watched rise from his home as a boy in West Seattle. In 1976 Ivar purchased the building. It turned out to be quite profitable for him—and due to the 14-foot-long, salmon-shaped wind sock he flew from the top after a long public battle with the city, a good means of promoting his restaurants as well.

Ivar was devoted to preserving the Seattle waterfront, which he deemed one of the city's greatest assets. On April Fools' Day 1953, four days before the Alaskan Way Viaduct opened, he hired a brass band to thank the city for creating "Acres of Covered Parking" for his Acres of Clams restaurant. In 1961, when the city refused to repaint a waterfront firehouse and threatened to decommission the fireboat *Alki*, which he could see from his office, Ivar fronted the funds required to repair them both. (There was a fight over whether the firehouse should be painted his "firehouse red" or the city's proposed "quiet russet-red.") He sang shoreline and fishing ballads on the radio, promoting the area, and decorated the streets near Puget Sound with flower baskets, as we still do today. Combined with the money he constantly donated to the city toward improving the area, Ivar's waterfront volunteerism earned him the moniker "Mr. Waterfront." When Ivar died in 1985, half of his estate went to the business school at the University of Washington, and half to the school of restaurant management at Washington State University.

Today, we keep his spirit alive by keeping things light—did you hear we're installing a drive-through fish bar in the Alaskan Way tunnel in 2023 to feed commuters stuck in traffic?—and using our mussels as a growing corporation to sustain and improve the communities that support us.

"A gullible bird waited for a handout at Pier 54 where Ivar Haglund, restaurateur, had posted a notice of welcome. The sign was in response to another waterfront sign that urges the public to refrain from feeding the gulls. 'They are beautiful, useful scavengers,' Haglund said, adding he hoped the public would feed whatever birds showed up outside his restaurant: 'The sea gulls, ducks and even the pigeons,' he said. 'You can't discriminate.' "

—RICHARD S. HEYZA, *SEATTLE TIMES*, NOVEMBER 9, 1971

Ivar Haglund feeding his gull friends.

Ivar at the new Salmon House, 1970.

CHAPTER 3
ENTRÉES

Sole food for the main event

Sautéed Clams   82

Grilled Halibut Cheeks
with Cherry Chutney   83

Cedar-Plank Sockeye Salmon
with Hazelnut Vinaigrette   84

Possession Sound Seafood Stew   87

Blackened Lingcod with
Onion Rémoulade   89

Chris Garr's House-Made
Bacon-Wrapped Halibut   90

Marsala-Steamed Mussels and Clams   93

Penn Cove Mussels in Thai Red
Curry Broth   97

Poached Halibut with Lemon
Dill Sauce   98

Breaded Razor Clams with
Jalapeño-Ginger Tartar Sauce   99

Linguine with White Clam Sauce   101

Quilcene Oyster Pan Roast   102

Shrimp Newburg   103

Crab Louie with San Juan
Island Dressing   104

Buttermilk-Fried Washington Smelt   109

Pan-Fried Trout with Apple Currant
Chutney and Garr's House-Made
Bacon   111

Copper River Penne Pasta with
Marinara Cream Sauce   114

Alder-Grilled King Salmon   115

Grilled Copper River King Salmon with
Champagne Tarragon Vinaigrette   118

Ivar's Crispy Fish Tacos   120

Fish-and-Chips Aplenty   123

*I*n this chapter, we net an all-star cast from the past—dishes like Poached Halibut with Lemon Dill Sauce, Shrimp Newburg, and Quilcene Oyster Pan Roast—and throw them in the hold with the most popular entrées on the menus at Ivar's today. If Ivar Haglund were still with us, he'd make a run for Chris Garr's House-Made Bacon-Wrapped Halibut, but he might also be curious to try our home version of Fish-and-Chips Aplenty, made not with traditional wheat flour, but with a crisp combination of rice and chickpea flours. He'd be thrilled by the rich flavor of the salmon Ivar's now uses for Grilled Copper River King Salmon with Champagne Tarragon Vinaigrette, and he'd surely flop over Ivar's Crispy Fish Tacos.

Now, we know not everyone cooks with his turbot jets on. Ivar's entrées aren't complicated, but we're not talking about food that just skates by. Please remember to prepare your eaters for a gillful of good smells. At the Salmon House, the Native American cedar racing canoes, carved totem poles, and the swimming salmon suspended above the dining room are entertaining enough to keep a person clam waiting for a meal. (Ditto for the antiques and model fireboats at Acres of Clams, and the stunning view from Mukilteo Landing.) At least, they're all interesting until the kitchen starts to smelt good. Since most home cooks aren't equipped with such distractions, you might consider adding a bit of historical décor to your home when you cook one of Ivar's favorites. It will decrease your chances of getting attacked by hungry sharks by 59 percent.

Sautéed Clams

We get our clams from families who have harvested them for generations from Puget Sound, like the Taylors and the Jeffords. They're delivered early each morning after harvest, which means they're cooked within hours after they're plucked from the water. Eating them doesn't take nearly as long. (Don't worry; the International Pacific Free Style Amateur Clam Eating Contest Association no longer holds its annual clam-eating contest, so you won't be timed or photographed.) We think the very best way to eat clams is with two hands and a great piece of bread. When you make these, have the bread ready and the table set, so you can dig in right when the clams are hot.

SERVES 2

2 tablespoons unsalted butter

½ cup ⅛-inch-thick matchsticks yellow onion

½ cup ⅛-inch-thick matchsticks carrots

½ cup ⅛-inch-thick matchsticks celery

2 teaspoons minced shallots

2 teaspoons minced garlic

1 teaspoon minced fresh thyme

1 teaspoon minced fresh flat-leaf parsley

1 teaspoon minced fresh basil

½ teaspoon freshly squeezed lemon juice (Meyer preferred)

2 pounds Manila clams, rinsed and scrubbed

⅓ cup dry white wine, plus additional for tasting

Kosher salt

Freshly ground black pepper

1 scallion, thinly sliced

Lemon wedges (Meyer preferred), for serving

For directions on how to clean clams, see page 71.

1. Melt the butter in a large skillet over high heat. Add the onion, carrots, celery, shallots, and garlic and cook until softened, about 7 minutes, stirring frequently. Add the thyme, parsley, basil, lemon juice, clams and wine (pour yourself a glass while you're at it) and cover. Cook until the clams open, about 5 minutes. (Discard any unopened clams.) Season to taste with salt and pepper and transfer to serving bowls. Sprinkle with the scallions and serve hot with the lemon wedges.

Why We KEEP CLAM

In 1985, Terry Heckler, who created the Running Rainiers, our Dancing Clams, and many other ad campaigns of repute throughout Seattle, used his graphic skill to turn the *A* upside down in "Keep Clam," the company motto. Why? Ivar's wanted to build a reason to Keep Clam right into the logo itself. And since it's now recognized around the world, we think it worked—even if that little twist does get a few (less clam) people steamed up.

Grilled Halibut Cheeks with Cherry Chutney

Halibut can be very big fish, sometimes weighing hundreds of pounds, which means inside the head of each fish, there are two very big cheeks—and inside each cheek is a secret pocket of tender, succulent flesh. In the spring, during halibut season, the cheek meat comes to market, and our chefs go *wild*. Grill them, as we do at Ivar's, and pair them with a simple chutney made with sweet Rainier cherries. If you feel like being cheeky, make everyone at your dinner table say "cheeks with cherry chutney" ten times fast before picking up a fork.

SERVES 4

1. In a large saucepan combine the cherries, onion, bell pepper, jalapeño, wine, brandy, honey, vinegar, and mirin. Bring to a boil, then lower the heat and simmer until the mixture is thickened and sweet, about 45 minutes. Stir in the basil and season to taste with salt and pepper. Let cool.

2. Oil the grill rack and preheat a gas or charcoal grill to high heat. Put two skewers through each halibut cheek parallel to each other. Brush the cheeks with the oil and season to taste with salt and pepper. Grill the cheeks for 3 to 4 minutes without turning, or until cooked through.

3. Serve with a generous spoonful of chutney alongside the fillet.

Fishing for Names

When Justin Bieber visited Ivar's, he ordered grilled king salmon. Ditto for Dale Chihuly, whose glass studio spent decades next to our Salmon House, and for David Hasselhoff. *Grey's Anatomy* was filmed from Acres of Clams (when the ferry crashed at the end of season 3), and our guest list includes Bono and Jeff and Beau Bridges (aka *The Fabulous Baker Boys*). And who could forget Wayne Cody?

What can we say? We like to reel in the big fish.

SPECIAL EQUIPMENT: 8 bamboo or metal skewers (if using bamboo, submerge in water and soak for 30 minutes before using)

• • • • • • •

1½ pounds Rainier cherries, stemmed, and pitted and coarsely chopped (about 3 cups)

1 large Walla Walla onion, cut into ¼-inch dice

½ red bell pepper, cored, seeded, and cut into ¼-inch dice

½ jalapeño, seeded and minced

¼ cup dry white wine

¼ cup brandy

¼ cup honey

¼ cup white wine vinegar

2 tablespoons mirin (sweet Japanese rice wine)

1 tablespoon chopped fresh basil

Kosher salt and freshly ground black pepper

4 halibut cheeks (about 1½ pounds total), unpinched

2 tablespoons canola or other vegetable oil, plus additional for oiling the grill rack

Cedar-Plank Sockeye Salmon with Hazelnut Vinaigrette

For centuries, natives of the Pacific Northwest roasted salmon on planks carved from the same cedars that provided material for their canoes, houses, and clothes. Before modern cooking techniques, the plank served as both cooking vessel and dinner plate. What our modern dining habits can't replace is the sweet, smoky flavor that cooking on a cedar plank provides—which is why Ivar's Salmon House still roasts salmon over an alder grill in the middle of the restaurant all the time.

SERVES 4

SPECIAL EQUIPMENT: Cedar grilling plank*

FOR THE VINAIGRETTE:

2 tablespoons white wine vinegar

1 tablespoon minced shallots

1½ teaspoons Dijon mustard

1½ teaspoons honey

¼ teaspoon freshly squeezed lemon juice (Meyer preferred)

⅓ cup hazelnut oil

¼ cup canola or other vegetable oil

1 tablespoon finely chopped toasted hazelnuts

1 teaspoon minced fresh flat-leaf parsley

Kosher salt and freshly ground black pepper

• • • • • • •

2-pound sockeye salmon fillet with skin

1 to 2 tablespoons extra-virgin olive oil

1 to 2 teaspoons salmon seasoning or rub

Use any leftover vinaigrette on a green salad.

1. Soak the grilling plank in water to cover for 2 hours, keeping it immersed. (Setting a can of beans on the plank works well.) Next, preheat a gas grill to medium-low heat.

2. To make the vinaigrette, in a food processor or blender, whirl the vinegar, shallots, mustard, honey, and lemon juice until smooth. With the motor running, slowly add the oils, processing until well combined, then transfer the mixture to a small bowl. Whisk in the hazelnuts and parsley and salt and pepper to taste. (If you're a luddite, whisk together the vinegar, shallots, mustard, honey, and lemon juice in a small bowl. Whisking constantly, very slowly add the oils, mixing until the vinaigrette is thickened, before whisking in the hazelnuts, parsley, salt, and pepper.)

3. Brush the salmon with the oil and sprinkle with the seasoning. Place the fillet on the plank, skin side down, and put the plank in the center of the grill. Cover and cook on the grill until just cooked through, with the lid closed, about 10 to 15 minutes, or until the internal temperature reads 135 degrees F on an instant-read thermometer. Serve right on the plank, with the vinaigrette drizzled on top.

*What Wood You Buy?

Omar Field, Ivar's director of purchasing (he started washing dishes on Pier 54 in 1973), isn't a fan of the high price kitchen stores charge for cedar cooking planks. He heads down to his local Dunn lumberyard and buys sections of untreated cedar siding. Cut them into salmon-size sections, and your wallet won't have to walk the plank for what amounts to a glorified stick.

Possession Sound Seafood Stew

Unlike our more casual, comforting chowders, this tomato-saffron stew is a fancier crowd-pleaser. Created by Steve Anderson in our Mukilteo restaurant, it also happens to be perfect for entertaining. Make the broth ahead (even a day or two), and then just reheat and add the seafood right before serving.

SERVES 4 TO 6

1. To make the broth, in a large saucepan, heat the oil over medium-high heat. Add the onion, carrots, and fennel bulb and fronds. Cook, stirring occasionally, until the vegetables start to brown, about 10 to 12 minutes. Stir in the parsley, garlic, orange zest, bay leaf, thyme, and saffron. Add the wine and anisette and simmer for 10 minutes. Stir in the tomatoes with their juice, clam juice, cayenne, salt, and pepper, and bring to a boil. Reduce the heat and simmer for 1 hour, uncovered.

2. Add the clams and mussels. Cook until they are almost all open, about 3 minutes. Stir in the prawns, crab, salmon, halibut, and scallops and cook for 3 to 5 minutes longer, or until the fish is cooked and the crab is warm. (Discard any clams and mussels that have not opened.) Ladle the stew into shallow bowls and serve with a piece of toasted garlic bread floating in each bowl, and a bib for each diner.

FOR THE BROTH:

3 tablespoons extra-virgin olive oil

1 large yellow onion, chopped

3 cups chopped carrots (1 pound, or about 7 medium)

1 medium fennel bulb, chopped

¼ cup chopped fennel fronds

¼ cup chopped fresh flat-leaf parsley

5 to 6 cloves garlic, minced

2 teaspoons finely grated orange zest

1 bay leaf

5 sprigs fresh thyme

1 teaspoon saffron threads

1 cup white wine

¼ cup anisette or other licorice-flavored liqueur

1 (28-ounce) can plus 1 (14-ounce) can diced tomatoes in juice

8 cups clam juice

¼ teaspoon cayenne pepper

½ teaspoon freshly ground black pepper

1 teaspoon kosher salt

• • • • •

1 pound Manila clams, rinsed and scrubbed

1 pound mussels, scrubbed and debearded

8 jumbo prawns, peeled and deveined

4 cooked snow crab legs

¼ pound skinless salmon fillet, cut into 1-inch pieces

¼ pound skinless halibut fillet, cut into 1-inch pieces

¼ pound bay scallops

12 slices toasted garlic bread

This recipe requires a very large pot (at least 6 quarts). Anything smaller, and the fish will be swimming right across your stovetop.

Blackened Lingcod with Onion Rémoulade

Despite the name, Pacific lingcod aren't cod—they're uglier fish, for one, so of course the cod family would reject them. On the plate, though, lingcod are gorgeous. Their flesh is delicate, with a sweetness unusual in white-fleshed fish. Seared and served with a sauce made with caramelized onions, they make a great supper for guests. Just be careful—those guests might fish for another invitation.

SERVES 4

1. Heat 1 tablespoon of the oil in a small skillet over medium-high heat. Add the onion and sugar and cook, stirring occasionally, until the onions are golden brown, about 20 to 30 minutes. Let cool. Transfer to a cutting board and finely chop.

2. In a medium bowl, combine the mayonnaise, pickle, mustard, capers, tarragon, anchovy paste, lemon juice, garlic, parsley, and basil and mix well. Stir in the onions and season to taste with salt and pepper. Set aside.

3. Prepare one recipe Three-Cheese Polenta (page 138). Keep the polenta in its pot, in a warm place, until ready to serve.

4. To cook the lingcod, sprinkle both sides of the fish with the blackening spice. Heat the 2 tablespoons of oil in a large non-stick skillet over medium-high heat. Add the fish and cook skin side up until browned, 3 to 4 minutes. Turn and cook for another 3 to 4 minutes, or until just cooked through. Serve next to warm polenta with the rémoulade on the side or dolloped on top.

Use any leftover rémoulade as a sandwich spread—think salmon and arugula on Macrina's sourdough.

FOR THE RÉMOULADE:

1 tablespoon extra-virgin olive oil

½ large Walla Walla or other sweet onion, thinly sliced

½ teaspoon sugar

1 cup mayonnaise

2 tablespoons minced dill pickle

4 teaspoons Dijon mustard

1 tablespoon drained, chopped capers

1 teaspoon minced fresh tarragon

1 teaspoon anchovy paste

1 teaspoon freshly squeezed lemon juice (Meyer preferred)

1 teaspoon minced garlic

½ teaspoon minced fresh flat-leaf parsley

½ teaspoon minced fresh basil

Kosher salt and freshly ground black pepper

• • • • • • •

1 recipe Three-Cheese Polenta (page 138)

• • • • • • •

Four 6- to 7-ounce lingcod fillets with skin

1 to 2 tablespoons blackening or creole spice

2 tablespoons extra-virgin olive oil

Chris Garr's House-Made Bacon-Wrapped Halibut

Our flounder went to great lengths to find the best fish in the sea, both before Ivar's opened, when he ran Seattle's first aquarium, and after, when he scoured the ocean for great fish and shellfish. (The theme also applied to his staff, but he didn't usually find them at the bottom of the ocean, and he hired only women for the front of the house.)

In his honor, we do the same today (with the fish, not the staff), making our own bacon in house and selecting the best halibut we can find from Pacific waters. This dish is a combination of those two favorites: a perfectly cooked halibut fillet hugged by a few slices of bacon, then drizzled with a sherry vinaigrette. Serve it with Roasted Fingerling Potatoes (page 150) and Sautéed Spinach (page 142).

SERVES 4

1½ cups dry sherry

1 bay leaf

3 black peppercorns

2 sprigs fresh thyme

¼ cup honey

2 tablespoons freshly squeezed lemon juice (from 1 medium lemon, Meyer preferred)

1 tablespoon Dijon mustard

¾ cup plus 2 tablespoons canola or other vegetable oil, divided

Kosher salt and freshly ground black pepper

Four 6-ounce halibut fillets, skinless

12 thin strips store-bought or Garr's House-Made Bacon (page 131)

1. In a small saucepan combine the sherry, bay leaf, peppercorns, and thyme and bring to a boil over high heat. Simmer until reduced to a syrup (about ¼ cup), about 15 minutes. Strain and let cool. Transfer to a food processor along with the honey, lemon juice, and mustard. With the motor running (head out on the highway!), slowly add ¾ cup of the oil, processing until well combined. Season to taste with salt and pepper and set aside.

2. Preheat the oven to 350 degrees F.

3. Season the halibut with salt and pepper to taste and wrap the bacon around the halibut, 3 strips per fillet, like a towel after a swim, securing it with toothpicks (the bacon, not the towel). Heat the remaining 2 tablespoons of oil in a large ovenproof skillet over high heat and add the halibut. Cook on one side for 2 to 3 minutes, or until the bacon is nicely browned. Turn the fish, place the pan in the oven, and roast for another 6 to 8 minutes, or until the halibut is just cooked through. Transfer to plates and serve drizzled with the vinaigrette.

Marsala-Steamed Mussels and Clams

In 2009 Miller High Life announced it was going to air the shortest Super Bowl ad in history, at just one second long. Not to be outdone, Ivar's ran a half-second ad. The commercial—just the Ivar's logo paired with a curious seagull and a high-pitched squawk announcing the restaurant's name—made waves in Seattle and was covered across the country. Here's a super bowl of shellfish that will last longer than that ad, but maybe not by much.

SERVES 2

1. Oil the grill rack and preheat a gas or charcoal grill to medium-high heat. Brush the onion slices on both sides, using about 1 tablespoon of olive oil. Place the onions and sausages on the grill, cover, and cook for about 10 minutes with the lid closed, turning the onions and sausage two or three times, until the onions are soft and charred in spots (arctic charred, if you prefer) and the sausage is browned on the outside and almost cooked through in the center.

2. Heat ¼ cup of olive oil in a large skillet over medium-high heat. Add the mussels and clams and cook, uncovered, stirring occasionally, until they start to open, about 3 to 4 minutes. Meanwhile, roughly chop the onions and set aside. Cut the sausage lengthwise, then cut each half into ¼-inch-thick half moons. Set the sausage aside. Add the garlic, shallot, thyme, and parsley to the shellfish and cook for 30 seconds. Add the marsala and cook for 1 minute, until it reduces by about a third. Add the chopped onions, chopped sausage, and butter, season to taste with salt and pepper, and cook for 3 more minutes, or until the butter has melted and all the clams and mussels have opened. (Discard any that do not open.) Serve with the broth in shallow bowls.

1 medium onion, cut into ¾-inch rounds

¼ cup extra-virgin olive oil, plus about 1 tablespoon for grilling

1 large or 2 small mild Italian pork sausages (about ½ pound)

1 pound Penn Cove mussels, scrubbed and debearded

1 pound Manila clams, rinsed and scrubbed

8 cloves garlic, peeled and well smashed

1 shallot, minced

4 sprigs fresh thyme

¼ cup chopped fresh flat-leaf parsley

⅔ cup marsala wine

¼ cup (½ stick) unsalted butter, cut into pieces

Kosher salt and freshly ground black pepper

Mark on Pier 54 playing Ivar's old guitar.

TOP: Richard Watson was crowned champion by Ivar Haglund in 1949, with a congratulatory handshake from Joe Silva.
BOTTOM: In 1952, Dick Taylor, second from the right, was the winner. Can you spot Miss Halibut Cheeks?

A Whale of a Contest

In 1947 the International Pacific Free Style Amateur Clam Eating Contest Association (IPFSACECA) announced that the first international clam-eating contest (aka the Seattle Clam Bowl) would be held on Pier 54. The inaugural bout featured Seattle's Dick Watson, a taxi driver who claimed he quenched his morning thirst with a quart of Ivar's Legendary Clam Nectar (see page 146) each day. The next year, he chowed down against Joe Silva, a truck driver from Martha's Vineyard and the crowned Atlantic Coast Champion. In 10 minutes of uninterrupted clam eating, the Seattleite won, but lost his title the next year to Brooklynite Joe Gagnon. The contest was only held six times.

These are the original International Pacific Free Style Amateur Clam Eating Contest Association rules:

1947 CLAM-EATING CONTEST O-FISH-AL RULES

#1 A contest consists of one 10-minute round of uninterrupted clam eating.

#2 Each contestant shall have an official clam counter whose duty is to count each clam eaten by the contestant. In the IPFSACECA the word eaten means taken in the mouth so the lips can be closed, and at the final bell all clams in the mouth with the lips closed qualify in the official and final count. A clam cannot be both in the mouth and out of it, it's got to be in so lips can be closed.

#3 The clam counter is to watch that each clam is eaten, adequately. An empty shell with no clam in it does not count as a clam consumed.

#4 The clams used in the contest shall be steamed littleneck clams from the Pacific Northwest, beach run. The clams shall be warm, not cold, nor shall the clams be too hot to impede fast handling. Clams shall be eaten on a catch-as-catch-can basis.

#5 There shall be an official timer with a stop watch for each contest, and at intervals throughout the contest an official clam count shall be called out so that contestants and spectators shall hear and know the score.

#6 All contestants and judges must signify the willingness to submit to the saliva test and the lie detector. The ethics and standards of the IPFSACECA are and always will be absolutely above reproach, questions, or shadow of suspicion.

#7 Any contestant or judge bringing ill repute or question to any contest or the IPFSACECA shall be dealt with in a manner to bring him ignominious humiliation. This should be sufficient warning to would-be fixers and cheap tinhorn gamblers. We believe firmly in fair play, justice, decency, and 100 percent true clam eating sportsmanship.

Penn Cove Mussels in Thai Red Curry Broth

Serve these mussels to a crowd with bread for dipping, or as a weeknight dinner with the broth and shellfish ladled over heaping bowls of jasmine rice. We get many of our mussels from the Jefferds family at Penn Cove Shellfish. Its operations, in Coupeville, Washington, on Whidbey Island are worth a visit when you're in the Pacific Northwest.

SERVES 2

1. In a large saucepan over medium-high heat combine the coconut milk, sake, curry paste, garlic, shallot, lime juice, and fish sauce. Bring to a boil, whisking together, then add the mussels. Cover, reduce the heat, and simmer until the mussels open, about 3 to 5 minutes. (Discard any that do not open.) Season to taste with salt and pepper. Serve with the broth in shallow bowls, sprinkled with the cilantro.

1 (15-ounce) can coconut milk, stirred to blend

½ cup sake

2 tablespoons Thai red curry paste

1 tablespoon minced garlic

1 medium shallot, minced

1 tablespoon freshly squeezed lime juice

1 tablespoon fish sauce

2½ pounds Penn Cove mussels, scrubbed and debearded

Kosher salt and freshly ground pepper

1 to 2 tablespoons chopped fresh cilantro

Use Your Mussels

Imagine, for a moment, that your beard was connected to your home. It would be uncomfortable, to say the least. But keep clam—the only creature that suffers that misfortune is the salty bivalve we call the mussel. The mussels' beards, technically called byssus threads, are indeed what connects them to their habitats. Although both wild and farmed mussels have them, the beards are often bigger—shaggier, if you will—when the mussels come from the wild. In either case, you'll need to "debeard" your mussels. First, scrub the shells under cold running water, discarding any that are broken or refuse to close when tapped. Just before cooking, use your thumb and first finger to grasp the beard and pull sharply, perpendicular to the mussel, to remove it. It's no harder to remove than a fake Santa's beard.

Linguine with White Clam Sauce

Near the ceiling of the Clam Digger Lounge inside Ivar's Acres of Clams, you'll see Ivar's collection of vintage clam-digging tools—everything from a giant six-tined clam fork to a rifle fitted with a white enamel shovel. While you are waiting for your ferry to Bainbridge Island, it's the best place to enjoy our linguine with clam sauce along with a bite of history—unless, of course, you decide to dig in at home. In that case, we recommend using a smaller fork.

SERVES 4

1. To make the pasta, bring a large pot of salted water to a boil over high heat.

2. Meanwhile, heat the oil in a large skillet over medium heat. Add the shallots and garlic and cook until softened, about 2 minutes. Add the clams, oregano, and red pepper flakes and cook, stirring, for 2 minutes. Add the clam broth and wine and bring to a boil. Cover and cook for 3 minutes, or until the clams open. Transfer the clams to a large bowl (discard any that have not opened) and cover to keep warm. Cook the liquid at a simmer until reduced by half and nicely flavored, 6 to 8 minutes. Add the butter and stir until melted. Season to taste with salt if needed.

3. Cook the pasta until it is just al dente, about 3 minutes. Drain and divide among 4 serving bowls. Top with the clams, pour the sauce over, and serve.

⅓ cup extra-virgin olive oil

¼ cup minced shallots

4 teaspoons minced garlic

2 pounds petite Manila clams, rinsed and scrubbed

4 teaspoons chopped fresh oregano

1 to 2 teaspoons crushed red pepper flakes

1 cup clam juice or Ivar's Legendary Clam Nectar (page 146)

1 cup dry white wine

½ cup (1 stick) unsalted butter, cut into ½-inch pieces

Kosher salt

1½ pounds fresh linguine or fettuccine

Ivar keeping clam, 1977.

Quilcene Oyster Pan Roast

Traditionally, a pan roast is so named because it's cooked in a pan, not because it's roasted—but the key is the cream, which gives the dish its signature richness. This 1950s Ivar's favorite relies on Quilcene oysters, harvested from a bay on the northeastern stretch of Washington's Hood Canal. They're known for their clean, mild flavor; it's no wonder the town of Quilcene is known as the "Pearl of the Peninsula."

SERVES 4

⅓ cup extra-virgin olive oil

¼ cup thinly sliced yellow onion

⅓ cup ⅛-inch-thick matchsticks celery

⅓ cup ⅛-inch-thick matchsticks carrots

4 teaspoons minced garlic

¾ cup heavy cream (be careful picking it up)

½ cup white wine

¼ cup chili sauce (American-style, not Asian-style)

1 tablespoon plus 1 teaspoon Worcestershire sauce

1 tablespoon plus 1 teaspoon minced fresh thyme

1 tablespoon plus 1 teaspoon minced fresh parsley

½ teaspoon sweet paprika

2 (10-ounce) jars shucked oysters with juices, or 16 shucked Quilcene oysters (for shucking instructions, see page 28)

¼ cup (½ stick) unsalted butter, softened and cut into small pieces

Kosher salt and freshly ground black pepper

4 thick slices baguette, toasted

1. Heat the oil in a large skillet over medium-high heat. Add the onion, celery, carrots, and garlic and cook for 5 to 7 minutes, or until softened, stirring occasionally. Add the cream, wine, chili sauce, Worcestershire, thyme, parsley, and paprika and bring to a simmer. Stir in the oysters and their juices. When the edges of the oysters begin to curl, stir in the butter and season to taste with salt and pepper. Turn off the heat. Put the baguette slices in shallow bowls and ladle the pan roast over. Serve hot.

Ivar and a gull friend.

Shrimp Newburg

There are few dishes more decadent than Shrimp Newburg, a Yankee favorite that migrated west with America's "gourmet" dining culture. As the story goes, Newburg sauce was originally created at New York restaurant Delmonico's, by a sea captain named Ben Wenberg, who showed it to Delmonico's chefs as part of a lobster preparation. When relations between Wenberg and the restaurant management sailed into rough waters, no one kept clam. In the end, the restaurant kept the dish, but changed its name to Newburg, and it became famous. The shrimp version—every bit as rich, with butter, cream, and brandy—was a strong staple on dinner plates at Ivar's in its first few decades of operation.

SERVES 4

1. Melt the butter in a large skillet over medium-high heat. Add the shallots and cook for 2 minutes, stirring occasionally. Add the sherry and brandy and simmer, reducing the liquid by half, about 3 to 5 minutes. Add the cream, nutmeg, and cayenne and bring to a simmer. Stir in the shrimp and cook for 2 minutes, until almost cooked. In a small bowl, whisk ½ cup of the hot liquid into the egg yolks. Pour the mixture back into the skillet, stirring constantly. Warm the sauce but do not let it boil. Season to taste with salt and pepper and serve with the rice and lemon wedges.

¼ cup (½ stick) unsalted butter

¼ cup minced shallots

½ cup dry sherry

½ cup brandy

2 cups heavy cream

½ teaspoon freshly grated nutmeg

¼ teaspoon cayenne pepper

1¾ pounds jumbo shrimp (16 to 20 per pound), peeled and deveined, with tails left on

2 large egg yolks

Kosher salt and freshly ground black pepper

2 cups cooked white rice, for serving

Lemon wedges (Meyer preferred), for serving

A Wedge of Truth

At one point, Ivar's served a lemon wedge with each and every entrée that left the kitchen. Now we use so many lemons each year that we're investigating opening a lemon farm on Vashon Island in Puget Sound. What about that sour Seattle weather, you ask? Well, a professor at the University of Washington predicts we'll have a perfect climate for citrus by about 2030. We'll hire the sun to help us and put a good squeeze on the lemon market.

Crab Louie with San Juan Island Dressing

When Ivar Haglund bought a colored, full-page ad in the *Seattle Times* (see page 106) for the 1962 World's Fair (he operated a restaurant and gift store at the fair), it included lyrics to a new song, chirped to the tune of "My Bonnie Lies Over the Ocean." The lyrics promise that the combination of Ivar's clam chowder, oyster stew, fish fry, and Crab Louie, a dish popular nationwide at the time, would cure inclement weather. It was a finny promise, if you ask us, knowing Seattle weather the way we do, but we can't argue; that Crab Louie is a magical old recipe.

SERVES 2

3 large eggs

FOR THE DRESSING:

1 teaspoon red wine vinegar

1 teaspoon sugar

1 cup mayonnaise

⅓ cup chili sauce (American-style, not Asian-style)

2 tablespoons chopped dill pickles

1 tablespoon chopped red bell pepper

1 tablespoon minced scallion

1 tablespoon chopped fresh flat-leaf parsley

1 teaspoon Worcestershire sauce

1 teaspoon prepared horseradish (we hate being unprepared)

Kosher salt and freshly ground black pepper

• • • • • • •

12 ounces hearts of romaine (from 2 to 3 heads), chopped

6 thin slices cucumber

1 large tomato, cut into wedges

12 pitted kalamata olives

12 ounces picked-over cooked Dungeness crabmeat, drained

1 red bell pepper, cored, seeded, and thinly sliced crosswise

Lemon wedges (Meyer preferred), for serving

1. Put the eggs in a small saucepan with cold water to cover. Bring to a simmer, cook for 1 minute, and remove from the heat. Cover and let stand for 8 minutes. Drain, run under cold water, and peel. Slice two of the eggs in half lengthwise and set aside for the salad. Finely chop the other egg and set it aside for the dressing.

2. To make the dressing, in a medium bowl, combine the vinegar and sugar and stir until the sugar has dissolved. Add the remaining ingredients and the chopped egg, seasoning to taste with the salt and pepper.

3. To make the salad, line 2 plates with the lettuce. Arrange the sliced eggs, cucumber, tomatoes, olives, crab, and bell pepper on top. Serve the dressing on the side along with the lemon wedges.

Jimmie Moon introduces the family to watermelon.

Seattle Times, *April 8, 1962.*

Ivar's School of Fish

Since Ivar's opened 75 years ago, we've purchased our fish from the Pacific Northwest because we know it's the best-tasting, the freshest, and the safest for our natural environment. Even in 1975, Ivar Haglund wanted to teach his customers how to select the finest fish for cooking at home, so he ran a series of newspaper ads, starting with the one below.

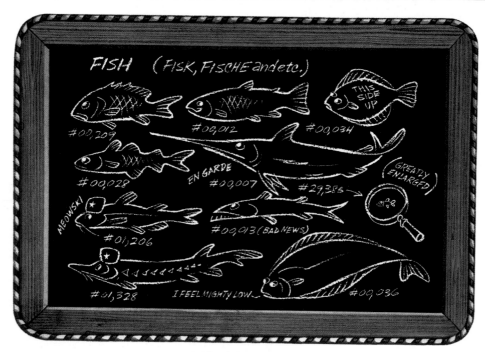

LESSON #1

There are 30,000 living species of fishes. This is enough to fill a menu at least twice the size of those featured at three of the Pacific Coast's leading seafood restaurants.

These are: (Take notes, there will be a test on Monday.)

Ivar's Acres of Clams; Ivar's Captain's Table; Ivar's Salmon House.

Fish served at Ivar's (and elsewhere, too) are so tasty because they live on a diet comprised mainly of seafood. This also keeps them healthy and svelte. You never hear a fish complaining, "Look at me! I can't go to the seashore looking like this!"

The Russians claim they caught the biggest salt water fish ever (a 3,250 pound sturgeon) and the biggest from fresh water too (a 564 pound catfish). There are those who say the Russians invented both claims, but in the interest of detente, who are we to argue?

The smallest fish known anywhere is the goby, found in Samoan waters. They weigh less than an ounce. Following a budget cut, they were featured at state dinners by John Haydon, governor of Samoa.

Class dismissed. (Feel free to use the tables down at Ivar's for your homework.)

Learnedly, *Ivar*

Ivar's INDIAN SALMON HOUSE
North Shore of Lake Union
at 401 NE Northlake Way
Phone 632-0767
Ample free parking

Ivar's CAPTAIN'S TABLE
Harborside
at 333 Elliott Avenue West
Phone 284-7040
Ample free parking

Ivar's ACRES OF CLAMS
Pier 54
at the foot of Madison Street
Phone 624-6852

Buttermilk-Fried Washington Smelt

In the early 1950s, smelt was on the menu at Ivar's for 65¢. Those were the days before smelt fell out of favor—and also before it fell back into favor. (We hake how that happens.) Today, smelt—really a family of tiny fish usually eaten whole, head and all—are available on and off throughout the entire year, depending on the location. Ask your local fishmonger to freeze some for you the next time there's a run; they thaw quickly, so you can call the store the morning you want to use them and have them ready to cook by dinnertime.

SERVES 4

1. Preheat the oven to 250 degrees F. Put the smelt in a large bowl and pour the buttermilk over. Heat 2 inches of oil in a Dutch oven or fryer over high heat until it registers 350 degrees F on a deep-fat thermometer.

2. Line a baking sheet with several layers of paper towels. Put the flour in a pie plate or shallow dish. Toss the smelt in the flour to coat. Shake off any excess and fry the fish 4 or 5 at a time until golden brown and crisp, 4 to 5 minutes. Transfer the smelt to the prepared baking sheet and keep warm in the oven while you fry the rest. Serve with the lemon wedges and tartar and cocktail sauces alongside.

1½ pounds whole smelt, rinsed

1 cup buttermilk

Canola or other vegetable oil, for frying

1 recipe Seasoned Flour (page 111)

Lemon wedges (Meyer preferred), for serving

Ivar's Famous Tartar Sauce (page 137), for serving

Ivar's Original Cocktail Sauce (page 136), for serving

Pan-Fried Trout with Apple Currant Chutney and Garr's House-Made Bacon

Fried on the stovetop in bacon fat and topped with our Apple Currant Chutney, this trout is the best way to prepare our region's inland river fish, next to grilling it over an open fire right next to the stream where you caught it. Serve it with Brown Sugar–Roasted Acorn Squash (page 145) and Salmon House Mesquite Cornbread Muffins (page 141).

SERVES 4

1. Cook the bacon in a large heavy skillet over medium-high heat until browned and crisp. Transfer to a paper towel–lined plate and keep warm. Put the flour in a pie plate or shallow dish.

2. Preheat the oven to 250 degrees F. Line a baking sheet with paper towels. Add a tablespoon of oil to the skillet. Dredge one trout in the flour and cook skin side up until browned, about 4 minutes. Turn and brown the other side, 1 to 2 minutes, or until the trout is just cooked. Transfer to the prepared baking sheet and place in the oven to keep warm while you repeat with the remaining oil and trout. To serve, top each trout with ½ cup of chutney and 2 bacon slices; sprinkle with scallions and serve.

 Ask your fishmonger to butterfly the fish for you. It's always best to reward the favor with a six-pack of Pike Pale Ale.

8 strips store-bought or Garr's House-Made Bacon (page 131)

1 cup Seasoned Flour (recipe follows)

¼ cup canola or other vegetable oil, divided

Four 1-pound trout, heads removed, boned, and butterflied

1 recipe Apple Currant Chutney (page 135)

1 scallion, thinly sliced

SEASONED FLOUR

MAKES ABOUT 2 CUPS

2 cups all-purpose flour

1 tablespoon kosher salt

1½ teaspoons freshly ground black pepper

1½ teaspoons dry mustard

1½ teaspoons sweet paprika

Pinch of cayenne pepper

¾ teaspoon chili powder

¾ teaspoon dried oregano

¾ teaspoon dried thyme

¾ teaspoon granulated garlic

¾ teaspoon onion powder

1. In a large bowl, whisk together all the ingredients.

Which Fish are You?

Two big things determine what salmon tastes like: where it comes from (denoted by a location, usually the name of a river, see page 114), and what species it is.

PINK salmon, aka humpback salmon, has pink flesh (surprise!). It's often used for canning; Ivar's doesn't serve pink very often.

SILVER salmon, aka coho, has pink-orange flesh with a flavor that's much lighter than that of both king and sockeye. Cohos weigh from 7 to 12 pounds and freeze very well compared to other species.

KING salmon, aka chinook, is known for its high fat content and rich taste. It has a dark orange color, and the fish itself is usually quite large (up to 50 pounds), hence the name. Because this is the least common of the salmon species, it's also often the most expensive.

SOCKEYE salmon, aka reds, have a deep red-orange flesh. They are often smaller fish, averaging 6 to 8 pounds, and have a distinct rich flavor.

CHUM salmon, aka keta, also has pink-orange flesh and a lighter flavor, and weighs 7 to 12 pounds on average. Because chum aren't usually as high in oil, they're best in preparations that bring in other flavors, like fish-and-chips or smoked salmon dishes.

Ivar didn't make the UW Huskies' football team.

A Handy Chart

Ivar's director of training Patrick Yearout developed a technique to teach new employees about the five kinds of wild Alaskan salmon using the shape of their hands. It's a "handy" way to remember which is which.

Don't forget the PINKie
SILVER on your ring finger
KING rules the hand
Don't poke your SOCKEYE out
Thumbs up for CHUM

Copper River Penne Pasta with Marinara Cream Sauce

When salmon hitch back upstream to freshwater from the ocean to spawn, they make a long, difficult trip inland, usually returning to the river they were born in. Since they don't eat once they enter freshwater (there's not great fast food in rivers these days), they must have huge stores of fat and oil to sustain them on their journey. There's a correlation between how each salmon tastes and which river it comes from: the longer and more difficult the return trip, the higher the fish's fat content, and therefore the silkier and richer the taste of its flesh. Copper River king salmon, the fish we use here, is one of the fattiest species (read: most flavorful).

SERVES 4 TO 6

FOR THE SAUCE:

2 tablespoons extra-virgin olive oil

2 large cloves garlic, minced

¼ cup vodka

1 (28-ounce) can diced tomatoes

¼ teaspoon red pepper flakes

2 tablespoons chopped fresh basil

Kosher salt and freshly ground
   black pepper

¾ cup heavy cream

• • • • • • •

1½ pounds penne or other short
   dried pasta

¼ cup extra-virgin olive oil

1 small fennel bulb, trimmed and
   thinly sliced

1 large yellow onion, thinly sliced

1 pound skinless Copper River king
   salmon, cut into 1-inch pieces

½ cup dry white wine

1 tablespoon chopped fresh flat-
   leaf parsley

1. To make the sauce, heat the oil in a large skillet over medium-high heat. Add the garlic and cook for 30 seconds. Add the vodka and cook until reduced by half, about 2 minutes. Stir in the tomatoes, pepper flakes, and basil and season to taste with salt and pepper. Simmer until reduced by half and flavorful, about 10 minutes. Add the cream and simmer for another 3 to 4 minutes, or until slightly reduced. Keep warm.

2. Bring a large pot of salted water to a boil over high heat. Add the penne and cook until still quite chewy, about 7 minutes. Drain and keep warm.

3. Heat the oil in a Dutch oven or other large saucepan over medium-high heat. Add the fennel and onion and cook until softened and lightly golden, about 10 minutes. Stir in the salmon and cook, stirring gently, until almost cooked through, about 3 minutes. (It will break up and stick to the pan, but that's fine.) Stir in the wine, simmer for 3 minutes, then stir in the sauce and the penne. Toss to coat and season to taste with salt and pepper. Divide among serving dishes, sprinkle with the parsley, and serve.

Alder-Grilled King Salmon

This simply grilled fish is what Ivar Haglund envisioned when he opened the Salmon House, with its 9-foot-long alder-fired grill in the middle of the dining room. At home, we recommend keeping clam by using your backyard grill and some seasoned alder chips. For a great aroma, throw a few branches of rosemary onto the coals just before you start grilling the salmon.

SERVES 4

1. Prepare the alder chips for smoking: Seal three or four big handfuls of chips in a disposable aluminum pan (with a sheet of heavy-duty aluminum foil as a cover) or a smoking box. Alternatively, you can place the chips on four 18-inch-long sheets of heavy-duty aluminum foil, wrap the chips up like a present, and poke 10 to 12 holes in the sides and top of the package with a skewer.

2. Spray the grill rack and preheat a gas or charcoal grill to high heat, with about ⅔ of the grilling area prepared for cooking over direct heat. If you are using a charcoal grill, light the charcoal; when it is glowing red, rake into two piles at opposite sides of the grill. If you are using a gas grill with 2 burners, preheat the grill to high on both burners and then turn off one burner. If you are using a gas grill with 3 burners, preheat the grill to high on all burners and then turn off one burner. (If you are using a grill with 4 burners, tell your chef to figure it out.) Place the package of alder chips over the hottest part of the grill, cover the grill, and wait for smoke to appear, between 10 and 20 minutes.

3. When the chips are smoking profusely, season the fillets to taste with salt and pepper. Place the fillets on the coolest part of the grill and cook, skin side down, without turning, for 10 to 20 minutes, or until the fish is just firm in the center. (Cooking time will depend on your grill and the thickness of your fillets, so be vigilant.) Brush with the butter and serve with the lemon wedges.

Nonstick cooking spray

Alder chips (about 3 big handfuls)

Four 7-ounce king salmon fillets with skin

Kosher salt and freshly ground black pepper

¼ cup (½ stick) unsalted butter, melted

Lemon wedges (Meyer preferred), for serving

At the Salmon House, we serve an Alder-Grilled Salmon Sampler, which allows customers to taste different varieties. To try this at home, purchase different types of salmon (king, coho, sockeye, etc.), blindfold your diners, and ask them to figure out which is which.

Note that thicker pieces of salmon require longer cooking times than thinner ones.

Smoke in the Air

As First Lady, Hillary Clinton requested 50 orders of Alder-Grilled King Salmon to be taken aboard Air Force One on her flight to the other Washington. It was the last time our food got protection from the Secret Service.

The 16-foot, 8-inch-tall welcoming man was carved for Ivar's in 2010 by David and Davey Boxley.

The Salmon House, Up in Smoke

After traveling throughout Asia, where it was common to see floating restaurants cater to customers arriving and departing by boat, Ivar Haglund decided in 1966 that he wanted to build a floating bathhouse in Ballard. Nick Nickerson, the real estate broker Ivar hired to find him a site, convinced Ivar instead to open a restaurant near the University of Washington, on the site of an old mill that once produced cedar shakes and shingles. The idea was sunk from the beginning; not only did his plans include building what he called "Ivar's Floating Restaurant" in the middle of an active boating channel, they also got snagged in the city's permitting process. In the end, Ivar decided that the land he'd originally purchased as the place to dock the restaurant, beneath Seattle's I-5 Bridge, was big enough for a new restaurant *and* great parking. Inspired by a visit to Tillicum Village, Ivar launched the concept of the Salmon House. He researched native cooking and design at the university's Burke Museum of Natural History and Culture, and eventually designed the restaurant after a traditional Native American longhouse.

On opening night in 1969, Ivar invited the Seattle Chamber of Commerce, city council, mayor, and the media to be the first to experience his delicious barbecued salmon dinner, which was to be cooked over the large alder fire in the center of the restaurant. We know now that alder has to be perfectly dry to burn correctly, but when the Salmon House opened, we weren't so bright. That first night, the restaurant filled with smoke as the damp alder hissed and crackled. (It didn't help that the Salmon House used the same circular exhaust holes that would have appeared in a Native American longhouse and not an exhaust fan.) Although no one was too upset that night, Ivar postponed the Salmon House's grand opening until 1970, when it launched with much success and very little smoke. Next time you visit, ask your server to show you the char marks in the restaurant's cedar beams.

"Totems, canoes, and carvings highlight the salmon, which our Puget Sound natives venerated long before we could pronounce polyunsaturated."

—IVAR HAGLUND, ON THE SALMON HOUSE

Grilled Copper River King Salmon with Champagne Tarragon Vinaigrette

In 2012 Ivar's bought 11,000 pounds of Copper River salmon. In the summer, when the weather's warm, grilled salmon is a Seattle staple (although it's probably safe to assume that most households don't order quite as much as we do). If you'd prefer to cook it indoors, you'll need two skillets, preferably cast-iron. Heat 2 tablespoons of olive oil in each skillet over medium-high heat and cook the salmon for 7 to 9 minutes, turning once. Serve this salmon with Roasted Fingerling Potatoes (page 150) or Steve's Strawberry Caprese Salad (page 58).

SERVES 4

Four 7-ounce Copper River king salmon fillets with skin

2 tablespoons canola or other vegetable oil, plus additional for oiling the grill rack

Kosher salt and freshly ground white pepper

FOR THE VINAIGRETTE:

2 tablespoons champagne vinegar

1 teaspoon honey

1 teaspoon Dijon mustard

⅓ cup plus 1 tablespoon extra-virgin olive oil

1 tablespoon chopped fresh tarragon

1. Oil the grill rack and preheat a gas or charcoal grill to medium heat. Brush the salmon with the vegetable oil and season to taste with salt and pepper. Set aside.

2. To make the vinaigrette, in a small bowl, whisk together the vinegar, honey, and mustard. Whisking constantly, very slowly add the oil, mixing until the vinaigrette is thickened. (If you like power tools, make this in a food processor or blender: Whirl the vinegar, honey, and mustard together until smooth. With the motor running, slowly add the oil, processing until well combined, then transfer the mixture to a small bowl.) Whisk in the tarragon and salt and pepper to taste.

3. Grill the salmon, skin side up, for 7 to 9 minutes, or until just opaque in the center, turning the fish just once, when it releases easily from the grill. Transfer the salmon to plates and serve drizzled with the vinaigrette.

Photo courtesy of Alaska Airlines.

Plane Good Salmon

You'll often see salmon on Ivar's menus defined by the river of their birth (and catch). Copper River king salmon, now famous for its high fat content, is one of our favorites. (We also love that we don't have to swim 280 miles to have our human babies.) It's so famous, in fact, Alaska Airlines painted one of its planes to look like the fish. Fittingly, on flights between Anchorage and Seattle, Ivar's chowder is sometimes served on this plane—the "Salmon-Thirty-Salmon."

Ivar's Crispy Fish Tacos

Ivar's is one of the nation's largest buyers of fresh cod, but it isn't all saved for fish-and-chips—we have a perpetual friendly battle among our chefs to create the best fish tacos. Created by chef Ray Espinoza, an employee since 1982, these fish tacos, which layer warm flour tortillas with romaine lettuce, salsa, *cotija* cheese, sour cream, fried cod, and a modern, Thai-inspired taco sauce, are one of our best sellers year after year.

SERVES 4

FOR THE SAUCE:

½ cup mayonnaise

¼ cup sriracha sauce

1 teaspoon hot sauce (more if you like your tacos spicy)

1 tablespoon seasoned rice vinegar

• • • • • • •

Canola or other vegetable oil, for frying

½ cup all-purpose flour

½ teaspoon kosher salt

¼ teaspoon freshly ground black pepper

12 ounces cod fillets, cut into 16 equal pieces

Eight 6-inch flour or corn tortillas, warmed

2 cups finely shredded romaine lettuce (from 1 head)

½ cup salsa

¼ cup cotija cheese*

3 tablespoons sour cream

1. To make the sauce, in a small bowl, whisk together all the ingredients.

2. Heat 2½ to 3 inches of oil in a large Dutch oven (preferably 6-quart) over medium-high heat until it registers 375 degrees F on a deep-fat thermometer. Line a baking sheet with several layers of paper towels. While the oil heats, stir together the flour, salt, and pepper on a pie plate or shallow dish. Coat the fish with the flour mixture and shake off any excess. Fry the cod in batches, turning, for 4 to 6 minutes each batch, until golden brown on the outside and just opaque in the center. Do not crowd the fish, keep the pieces turning, and keep the oil temperature at 375 degrees F. With a slotted spoon, transfer the fish to the prepared baking sheet as it finishes cooking.

3. Spread each tortilla with the taco sauce. Top with some lettuce, 2 pieces of fish, and a spoonful of salsa. Sprinkle with the cheese and add a drizzle of sour cream. Repeat with the remaining tortillas.

4. Enjoy the tacos with plenty of napkins; they're delightfully messy.

* Cotija cheese is a hard, crumbly cow's milk cheese used often in Mexican cooking. If you can't find it, substitute crumbled feta or shredded Monterey Jack cheese.

Fish-and-Chips Aplenty

On some original Ivar's menus, the fish-and-chips meals are described as "Fish and Chips A Plenty." Although we sell our fish-and-chips in various sizes today (two-piece, three-piece, four-piece, and five-piece), we love the idea of each customer always having just that: plenty! When it comes to cod, we sold almost 2 *million* orders of cod fish-and-chips in 2012—and that's not counting baskets filled with halibut, salmon, clams, and shrimp. *That's* plenty.

It might surprise you that instead of all-purpose flour, we use a mixture of rice and chickpea flours for a crisp finish on our fish. Keep clam, they're easy to find—just look in the specialty flour section of the baking aisle at most large grocery stores.

SERVES 4

1. Preheat the oven to 200 degrees F. Line a baking sheet with aluminum foil, set a wire rack on the foil, and place it in the oven.

2. Heat 2½ to 3 inches of oil in a large Dutch oven (preferably 6-quart) over medium-high heat until it registers 375 degrees F on a deep-fat thermometer. Meanwhile, in a medium bowl, whisk together the water, rice flour, chickpea flour, egg white, cornstarch, salt, and baking powder until smooth; set aside at room temperature.

3. Cut the potatoes into ⅜-inch sticks, each 3 or more inches long. Place them in a large bowl, cover with cold water, and stir them to release their starch. Let soak about 15 minutes. Drain the potatoes in a colander, rinse under cold running water, and dry them completely with kitchen towels. Fry the potatoes in batches in the hot oil, 8 to 10 minutes per batch, or until thoroughly browned. Do not crowd them, keep the potatoes turning, and keep the oil temperature at 375 degrees F. With a slotted spoon, transfer the cooked potatoes to the wire rack in the oven to drain and keep warm while you fry the rest.

4. Line another baking sheet with paper towels. Make sure the oil is still at 375 degrees F. Dip the fish into the batter and shake off any excess. Fry the fish in batches, turning once, for 4 to 6 minutes per batch, until golden brown on the outside and just opaque in the center. Do not crowd them and keep the oil temperature at 375 degrees F. With a slotted spoon, remove the fish and drain on the prepared baking sheet. Serve the fish immediately with the potatoes, malt vinegar, and tartar sauce.

Canola or other vegetable oil for deep-frying

½ cup water

⅓ cup plus 1 tablespoon rice flour

¼ cup chickpea flour

1 large egg white

2 tablespoons cornstarch

½ teaspoon kosher salt

¼ teaspoon baking powder

Four 7-ounce russet potatoes, peeled

1½ pounds cod fillets, cut into 12 two-ounce pieces

Malt vinegar

Ivar's Famous Tartar Sauce (page 137)

The Secret Cod

At an Ivar's fish bar, you'll hear our servers use a kind of shorthand with our cooks. Here's how to know how many orders of fish-and-chips a person wants:

Two	=	A Pair
Three	=	A Crowd
Four	=	A Bunch
Five	=	A Handful
Six	=	A Happening
Seven	=	A Bummer
Eight	=	A Nightmare

As in, "Gimme a bummer for the Ocsan family."

If you've ever had fish-and-chips on Pier 54, you've seen the friendly seagull squadron that devotes its days to cleaning up the pier for us. We're so thankful to our gulls that we've hired them to do some advertising for us. In 2016, after they complete years of training by Kirsten and Jay, our special Seagull Advertising Squadron will take to the skies, spelling out messages for the public in water vapor using Ivar's patented gull-training education system.

You're not that gullible, are you?

A SEATTLE FAVORITE SINCE 1938

Ivar Haglund's strong personality and media genius brought him and his restaurants a lot of attention. According to the *Port of Seattle Reporter*, his clam-eating contest, for example, got more press for Seattle worldwide in 1946 than the Husky football team, the Seattle Art Museum, and the University of Washington *combined*. Ivar's became not only a waterfront favorite, but also part of how Seattle was represented around the globe.

When Ivar's opened a booth at the Seattle World's Fair in 1962, the papers went wild, chomping at the hook. The press seemed thrilled at the prospect of Ivar's representing the Seattle food scene. "Visitors to Seattle should understand that Seattle has not always been a great eating town," wrote the *Seattle Post-Intelligencer* in May of the same year.

Today, Ivar's still represents Seattle. Sports lovers from around the world indulge in chowder and fish-and-chips when they visit Seattle's Safeco and CenturyLink fields, KeyArena, and the University of Washington's Husky Stadium. (In 2012 CenturyLink and Safeco Fields combined sold more than 60,000 cups of chowder, 20,000 pounds of cod, and 75,000 orders of fish-and-chips.) And though many Seattleites may not realize it, they're supporting Ivar's when they buy the stadiums' Grounders World Famous Garlic Fries, which Ivar's makes for one out of every 11 fans at our city's games. (It's the most popular ballpark food around—except with your spouse, who hates garlic.)

Ivar's is a Seattle museum—literally, if you peruse the vintage photographs inside any Ivar's restaurant, and figuratively, because digging deep into the restaurant's history reveals a parallel history of the Emerald City.

We couldn't be more proud.

Ivar's, 1953.

CHAPTER 4

SIDES & STAPLES

The little things that make Ivar's great

Garr's House-Made Bacon   131

Grays Harbor Cranberry Chutney   134

Apple Currant Chutney   135

Ivar's Original Cocktail Sauce   136

Ivar's Famous Tartar Sauce   137

Three-Cheese Polenta   138

Salmon House Mesquite
Cornbread Muffins   141

Sautéed Spinach   142

Roasted Celery Root and
Yukon Potato Hash   143

Brown Sugar–Roasted Acorn Squash   145

Ivar's Legendary Clam Nectar
(Clam Stock)   146

Spicy Coleslaw   149

Roasted Fingerling Potatoes   150

*I*t's no fish story that Ivar's sometimes thinks outside the cereal box; for 75 years, the restaurant has been known for finny business. Whale, here's the catch: Ivar's takes side dishes seriously. No gorgeously cooked slab of salmon would be happy without a bite of Sautéed Spinach or Roasted Fingerling Potatoes alongside, so each time our chefs take on an order, they pay attention to the whole plate. They make sure Three-Cheese Polenta is smooth and piping hot each time it leaves the kitchen, and that the Brown Sugar–Roasted Acorn Squash is always just sweet enough. Schools of customers depend on getting the same delicious Ivar's Original Cocktail Sauce and Ivar's Famous Tartar Sauce each time they arrive, so our recipes are tried and true. Here's where we pass them on to you.

And here's a secret, if you promise to keep clam: this chapter has a hidden brunch menu. For the ultimate Sunday morning, serve Garr's House-Made Bacon next to plates of Roasted Celery Root and Yukon Potato Hash, with poached eggs and Salmon House Mesquite Cornbread Muffins. It's morning sole food at its finest.

Garr's House-Made Bacon

Fish may be our business at Ivar's, but making bacon is a favorite hobby for chef Chris Garr. Here's the skinny on our house-made hog: it's the same stuff we use to wrap around halibut (see the recipe on page 90) and sprinkle over our Bacon and Blue Knife-and-Fork Salad (page 57), but you could also pair it with eggs in the morning or use it to make bacon-wrapped scallops. Just don't get all buttered up about eating it too quickly—it takes about a week to prepare.

MAKES 2½ POUNDS

1. In a small bowl, combine the salt, brown sugar, and curing salt and sprinkle over all surfaces of the pork belly. Wrap well and store in the refrigerator for 6 days, turning it over every day. (We normally advise tasting, but in this case, it's best to keep your paws off.) After 6 days, rinse the salt mixture off and place the pork on a rack set over a baking sheet. Leave unwrapped and refrigerate overnight. Pat dry and drizzle the top surface with the syrup.

2. Preheat a gas or charcoal grill to low heat, with about ⅔ of the grilling area prepared for cooking over indirect heat. If you are using a charcoal grill, pile the applewood chips in with the charcoal and light them all; when they are glowing red, rake them into a pile on one side of the grill. If you are using a gas grill, prepare the applewood chips for smoking: Seal three or four big handfuls of chips in a disposable aluminum pan (with a sheet of heavy-duty aluminum foil as a cover) or a smoking box. Alternatively, you can place the chips on four 18-inch-long sheets of heavy-duty aluminum foil, wrap the chips up like a present, and poke 10 to 12 holes in the sides and top of the package with a skewer. If your grill has 2 burners, preheat the grill to high on both burners. Place the chips on the grill and cook with the lid closed until they begin to smoke profusely, between 10 and 20 minutes. Turn off one burner and reduce the other to low heat. (If you are using a gas grill with 3 burners, preheat the grill to high on all burners, start the chips smoking, then turn off two of the burners and reduce one to low. In any case, you're aiming for a grill temperature of about 200 degrees F.)

3. Place the bacon on the grill, over the area with no direct heat, and smoke for 2 to 3 hours, or until the bacon registers 150 degrees F on an instant-read thermometer. Cool, cut off the skin and outer edges, and use the skin for another dish (discard the edges as they are super-salty). Thinly slice the bacon and fry in a skillet.

¼ cup kosher salt

3½ tablespoons packed light brown sugar

2 teaspoons pink curing salt

2½ pounds pork belly*

1 tablespoon maple syrup

Applewood chips (about 3 big handfuls)

*Ask your local butcher to order pork belly for you a few days ahead.

If you're using a hot smoker, smoke the bacon for about 12 hours.

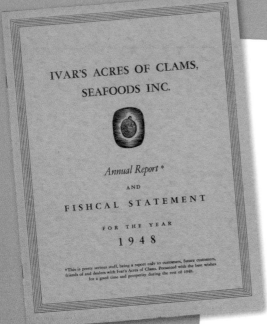

IVAR'S ACRES OF CLAMS,
SEAFOODS INC.

Annual Report *

AND

FISHCAL STATEMENT

FOR THE YEAR

1948

This is pretty serious stuff, being a report only to customers, future customers, friends of and dealers with Ivar's Acres of Clams. Presented with the best wishes for a good time and prosperity during the rest of 1949.

ORGANIZATION CHART

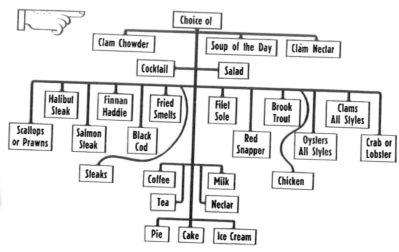

To accommodate our readers who prefer old-fashioned financial statements, we include this balance sheet. It is repeated from the 1948 report, on the odd complaint of our stockholders that one year wasn't long enough to figure it out.

Statement of Consolidated Balance Sheets, Parent Company

UNAMORTIZED DISCOUNT, EXPENSE AND SINKING FUND	$ 2,359,034.57
SUNDRY DEFERRED LIABILITIES, DEFERRED INCOME AND RESERVES AND LONG-TIME SKOOKUM	488,88.80
LESS ADJUSTMENT FOR INVESTMENT APPROPRIATION TO SUNDRY RESERVES OF AMOUNT EQUAL TO THE TAX BENEFIT RESULTING FROM THE OFFSET AGAINST CAPITAL GAINS OF THE OPERATING SKOOKUM IN THE CONSOLIDATED RETURN	9.03
UNDERLYING BOOK VALUE INTEGRAL TO RECEIVABLES, DIVIDENDS AND SERVICE SUBSIDIARIES	$ 11,2öl,†¶‡.‡0
ACCRUED SKOOKUM	(No Charge)
	$123,456,789,098

Fishcal Reports

In 1948 Ivar Haglund took out his first ad in the *Wall Street Journal*, which read: DUE TO THE ILLNESS OF MY AUNT, WE POSTPONED THE ANNUAL MEETING. THERE WILL BE NO DIVIDENDS UNTIL WE HAVE FOUND THE KEY TO THE PETTY CASH DRAWER. WRITE FOR THE FISHCAL REPORT. Of course, no businessman familiar with the *Journal* had ever heard of a "fishcal" report, and many wrote Ivar's to request one. True to his nature, Ivar had one on the hook, written by none other than his trusty auditor, Mr. Addington Diggit.

Of the auditing procedure, Ivar wrote, in the report's foreword:

> [Mr. Diggit] was not only unbiased about the company, but also about auditing. He had never tried it before. During the examination of our operations, we opened our books, our ovens and about a gunnysack of clams. We hid nothing but the cash register. At the conclusion of his examination he said he was well satisfied, or would be if he had just one more bowl of clams.
>
> We let him have it. After he finished the bowl, he said this reduction in our assets threw off all the figures, and he would have to re-audit the whole business the next day, at a somewhat higher fee for overtime.

The report was outrageous, filled with silly versions of what one might find in normal fiscal statements, like an organizational chart devoted to menu items instead of people, asset reports that included units of vitamin A on hand, and charts reporting how people's health improved when they ate more seafood. On employee relations, Ivar wrote, "How our employees get along with their relatives is their own business."

We can't help but wonder whether this sort of fishy reporting would fly in today's slightly more serious investment climate.

PEOPLE LIKE SEAFOOD

Out of 9½ customers who regularly order a bowl of Ivar's fresh steaming little neck clams with real melted butter, 9 do so because they like clams and know that they'll get the best ones at Ivar's. That last fellow throws away the meat and eats the shells, but he's only half there.

Grays Harbor Cranberry Chutney

Did you know Washington is the country's fifth-largest producer of cranberries? Near the same shores that produce oysters, mussels, and razor clams, our bogs boast some of the best berries . . . in the nation? In the universe? In history? In chutney!

Made with a mixture of cranberries, port, red wine, and spices, our cranberry chutney is delicious spooned into smooth soups, like Pink Banana Squash Soup (page 62). It would also be great with simply grilled halibut, or even as a substitute for traditional cranberry relish on the family Thanksgiving table.

MAKES 2 CUPS

SPECIAL EQUIPMENT: Cheesecloth, for tying spices

• • • • • • •

1 bay leaf

½ teaspoon black peppercorns

4 to 5 sprigs fresh thyme, or ½ teaspoon dried

1 cinnamon stick

1 star anise (triangle anise works just as well)

1 cardamom pod, crushed

⅔ cup red wine

½ cup port

½ cup apple juice

3½ tablespoons sugar

1 (12-ounce) bag fresh or frozen cranberries

½ teaspoon pure vanilla extract

Kosher salt

1. Wrap the bay leaf, peppercorns, thyme, cinnamon, star anise, and cardamom in a piece of cheesecloth, tie it tightly, and add to a medium saucepan along with the red wine and port. Bring to a boil and simmer until the liquid is reduced to ¼ cup, about 6 to 7 minutes. Add the apple juice and reduce by half, another 4 to 5 minutes. Stir in the sugar and cranberries and cook, stirring occasionally, until half the berries have popped, about 2 to 3 minutes. Remove and discard the spice bundle. Stir in the vanilla, season to taste with the salt, and let cool before serving.

The missing chef Ray Espinoza, now in Year 31 with Ivar's, preparing for a banquet.

Apple Currant Chutney

Developed for our Pan-Fried Trout with Apple Currant Chutney and Garr's House-Made Bacon (page 111), this Asian-inspired chutney is a nice blend of sweetness and spice—and since it uses Walla Walla onions and apples, it's about as Washington as you can get.

MAKES 2 CUPS

1. Combine all the ingredients except for the chives in a medium saucepan over high heat. Bring to a boil, lower the heat to a simmer, and cook, stirring occasionally, until reduced to a jam-like consistency, about 45 to 55 minutes. Stir in the chives and let cool. Serve at room temperature.

1 Fuji apple, peeled, cored, and chopped

¾ cup finely chopped Walla Walla or other sweet onion

¾ cup jarred Major Grey's mango chutney

⅔ cup currants

¼ cup finely chopped red bell pepper

⅓ cup unseasoned rice vinegar

⅓ cup water

2½ tablespoons mirin (sweet Japanese rice wine)

2½ tablespoons sugar

2 teaspoons minced pickled ginger

1 teaspoon *sambal oelek* or other Asian hot sauce

½ teaspoon finely grated lemon zest (Meyer preferred)

½ teaspoon ground allspice

2 teaspoons minced fresh chives

Scott Kingdon meeting with the Federal Aviation Administration to launch hot air balloons from the end of Pier 54 for Ivar. Paul Dorpat is the expert photographer.

Ivar's Original Cocktail Sauce

Nothing defines a fish restaurant like its cocktail sauce. Ours has been making buoys and gulls happy for three-quarters of a century. If you don't want to buy a jar at a Seattle-area grocer (QFC, Fred Meyer, and Town & Country Markets carry it), you can make it at home. Serve it with fresh-steamed prawns, Dungeness crab, or as a unique sauce on your favorite burger.

MAKES 1 CUP

¼ cup finely chopped yellow onion

1 tablespoon finely chopped green bell pepper

1 tablespoon prepared horseradish

¼ teaspoon sugar

¼ teaspoon kosher salt

¼ teaspoon hot sauce

⅔ cup chili sauce (American-style, not Asian-style)

2 tablespoons white vinegar

½ teaspoon Worcestershire sauce

1. Combine the onion, bell pepper, horseradish, sugar, salt, and hot sauce in a small food processor and process until finely chopped. Add the remaining ingredients and process for 15 seconds longer. Serve well chilled.

Ivar's cartoons ran from 1949 to 1961.

Ivar's Seafood Cookbook

Ivar's Famous Tartar Sauce

In his 2000 review of Safeco Field's ballpark fare, *Seattle Times* writer Ron Judd said that our tartar sauce would make even a two-by-four tasty. Ron's a rugged outdoorsman, but we haven't tried it on timber. Wood you?

For a springtime treat, add a tablespoon of Meyer lemon juice to the sauce and use it as a dip for steamed fresh asparagus. Tartar's not just for breakfast anymore!

MAKES 2 CUPS

1. Combine the onions, bell pepper, relish, vinegar, sugar, and salt in a food processor and process for 10 seconds. Add the mayonnaise and process for an additional 15 seconds. Serve chilled.

¼ cup chopped yellow onions

2 tablespoons chopped green bell pepper

2 tablespoons Pleasant Valley dill relish or other dill pickle relish

1 tablespoon white vinegar

1½ teaspoons sugar

½ teaspoon kosher salt

2 cups mayonnaise

Bob Hoheisel and Ruth Shields, circa 1955—What's he holding? Extra tartar sauce!

Three-Cheese Polenta

At our full-service restaurants, Ivar's serves this cheesy polenta warm and soft. You can do that too, but if you have extra, pour it into a small oiled dish and chill it overnight. In the morning, cut it into slices the size of a deck of cards, then fry the polenta cakes in butter and serve with poached eggs.

SERVES 4

8 cups water

1 tablespoon kosher salt

2 ¼ cups coarsely ground cornmeal

1 ¼ cups shredded Parmesan

½ cup shredded white cheddar

½ cup shredded orange cheddar (purple or green would also work)

¼ cup (½ stick) unsalted butter

1 to 3 teaspoons hot sauce

1 teaspoon freshly ground black pepper

¼ cup chopped fresh flat-leaf parsley or basil, or a combination

2 large eggs, lightly beaten

1. Combine the water and salt in a large saucepan over high heat and bring to a boil. Whisking constantly, steadily pour in the cornmeal. Cook, stirring frequently with a wooden spoon, until the mixture has thickened and pulls away from the side of the pan, about 20 to 30 minutes. Remove from the heat and stir in the remaining ingredients except the eggs. Remove 1 cup of the polenta to a medium bowl and gradually whisk the eggs into the polenta. Whisk the mixture back into the polenta, cook for 1 minute more, and serve warm.

 For a treat, dice some of Garr's House-Made Bacon (page 131) and stir it in just before serving.

In the 1950s, Ivar ran many of his ads as comic strips.

Retrieving Lost Treasure

The crack advertising and marketing department at Ivar's—which for years consisted of one Ivar Haglund—has long been known for its one-two punch: the ads almost always work, first, because people see them, and second, because the ads themselves tend to become news items.

Take the case of the underwater billboards. In August 2009 *Seattle Times* photographer Dean Rutz snapped photos of Ivar's raising a rusty billboard advertising Ivar's chowder from Elliott Bay, off Duwamish Head. Over the next month, the *Times*, along with most Seattle media, covered the attempt to authenticate the billboard.

The history goes something like this: In 1953 Ivar had been a member of the state transportation panel, which examined building a bridge from Seattle to Bainbridge Island. Ivar learned that the ferry system was considering building submarines, which were more efficient than boats, to move passengers, so Ivar rented locations from the Department of Fisheries to place billboards underwater for the sub commuters. In his research for a book on Ivar, noted Seattle historian Paul Dorpat had discovered the maps and drawings for the billboards, and even found canceled checks to lease the tidelands.

Of course, the entire thing was a hoax (even the photograph below showing the "raising" of the billboard), devised and executed by modern Ivar's leaders to make the company a news item. Ivar Haglund would have smelt the plan from the beginning, but by gull, he would have been proud.

Seattle's KING 5 covered the story on its *Evening Magazine* program. To see the footage of the billboard reveal, go to Ivars.com, click on History, then navigate to the TV/Radio links.

Salmon House Mesquite Cornbread Muffins

For many longtime Ivar's customers, the best start of a meal at the Salmon House is right after the drinks come, when the server sets a basket of steaming corn muffins on the table with butter and pots of honey—honey that, since 2012, has come straight from hives on top of the Salmon House.

The muffins get their sweet, smoky flavor from mesquite flour, which is made from the dried pods of a mesquite tree. Look for mesquite flour in the baking aisle of a well-stocked natural foods store, such as Puget Consumers Cooperative (PCC) or Whole Foods Market.

MAKES A DOZEN

1. Preheat the oven to 375 degrees F. Line 12 muffin cups with paper liners or grease the cups.

2. In a large bowl, whisk together the flour, mesquite flour, sugar, ¼ cup of the cornmeal, baking powder, and salt. In a small bowl, whisk the eggs lightly, then whisk in the butter and milk. Pour the wet ingredients into the dry ones and stir just until combined.

3. Divide the batter among the prepared muffin cups and sprinkle with the remaining tablespoon of cornmeal. Bake for 20 to 25 minutes, or until a toothpick inserted in the center comes out clean. Let the muffins cool in the tin for 5 minutes, then turn out onto a rack to cool further, or serve hot with butter and honey.

2 cups all-purpose flour

½ cup mesquite flour

½ cup sugar

¼ cup plus 1 tablespoon finely ground cornmeal, divided

1 tablespoon plus 1 teaspoon baking powder

1 teaspoon kosher salt

3 large eggs, at room temperature

1 cup (2 sticks) unsalted butter, melted

¾ cup milk, at room temperature

Ivar's Whalemaker Lounge in the Salmon House, 2013. Can you find the oosiks?

Sautéed Spinach

At Ivar's, we sauté spinach very quickly over super-high heat, so it's just barely wilted, then we serve it instantly, before it can release any liquid. If you want to make this recipe for more than one or two people, parboil the spinach first for a minute or two, plunge it in a bowl of ice water to stop the cooking, squeeze out the liquid, then cook the spinach a bit longer, about 3 minutes. Piled against grilled salmon and polenta, it makes a beautiful presentation—and it's tasty too!

SERVES 1 OR 2

2 tablespoons unsalted butter

2 tablespoons minced shallots

½ pound spinach leaves, trimmed

½ teaspoon kosher salt

½ teaspoon freshly ground black pepper

1. In a large skillet over high heat, melt the butter. Add the shallots and cook until softened, about 3 minutes. Stir in the spinach, salt, and pepper and cook, stirring, until the spinach is just wilted, about 1 to 2 minutes. Serve hot.

Roasted Celery Root and Yukon Potato Hash

Although this simple hash (and variations of it) appears on our dinner menu regularly, we think it will float your boat best in the morning as part of a Sunday brunch, in place of hash browns. Look for gnarly, bumpy celery root in the produce section of your local grocery—it's not pretty, but it has a lovely, gentle celery flavor. Peel it with a small, sharp knife.

SERVES 4

1. Preheat the oven to 350 degrees F. Toss the celery root and potatoes with 2 tablespoons of the oil and season to taste with salt and pepper. Spread in a single layer on a baking sheet and roast, turning once or twice, for 45 minutes, or until tender and browned. Toss the onion with another tablespoon of the oil, season to taste with salt and pepper, and add it to the pan with the other vegetables, turning to blend them all together. Roast until all the vegetables are tender and browned, about 20 minutes more. Combine all the vegetables in a large bowl with the parsley and the remaining tablespoon of oil and serve.

1 medium (about 1 pound) celery root, peeled and cut into 1-inch cubes
½ pound Yukon Gold potatoes, cut into eighths
¼ cup extra-virgin olive oil, divided
Kosher salt and freshly ground black pepper
½ Walla Walla or other sweet onion, chopped
¼ cup chopped fresh flat-leaf parsley

Francis Ramilo greets the Mimi C and Kerry Thomsen at Pier 54.

Brown Sugar–Roasted Acorn Squash

Each fall, when sweet, buttery acorn squash come straight from the fields to our chefs, we roast them as simply as possible; they need nothing more than a bit of butter and brown sugar. Add too much, and you'll squash out that natural earthy flavor.

SERVES 4

1. Preheat the oven to 400 degrees F. Line a baking sheet with foil or parchment paper. In a large bowl, toss the squash with the remaining ingredients and spread in a single layer on a baking sheet. Roast until tender when pierced with a fork, about 40 minutes.

2 acorn squash, about 1 pound each, quartered and seeded

¼ cup (½ stick) unsalted butter, melted

½ cup packed light brown sugar

Kosher salt and freshly ground black pepper

Ivar's Legendary Clam Nectar (Clam Stock)

Some folks say that seafood products have the power to make people more virile. We say there's only one way to find out.

MAKES 6 CUPS

3 pounds Manila clams, rinsed and scrubbed

8 cups water

1 cup chopped yellow onions (about 1 large)

1 cup chopped celery (2 to 3 ribs)

1 cup chopped carrots (about 1 medium)

1 bay leaf

3 black peppercorns

Kosher salt

1. Combine all the ingredients except the salt in a large saucepan and bring to a boil. Reduce the heat to a simmer and cook, uncovered, for 30 minutes. Strain the broth, reserving the clams, and season to taste with the salt.

Pier 54 fish bar, 2013. See page 137 for an earlier version.

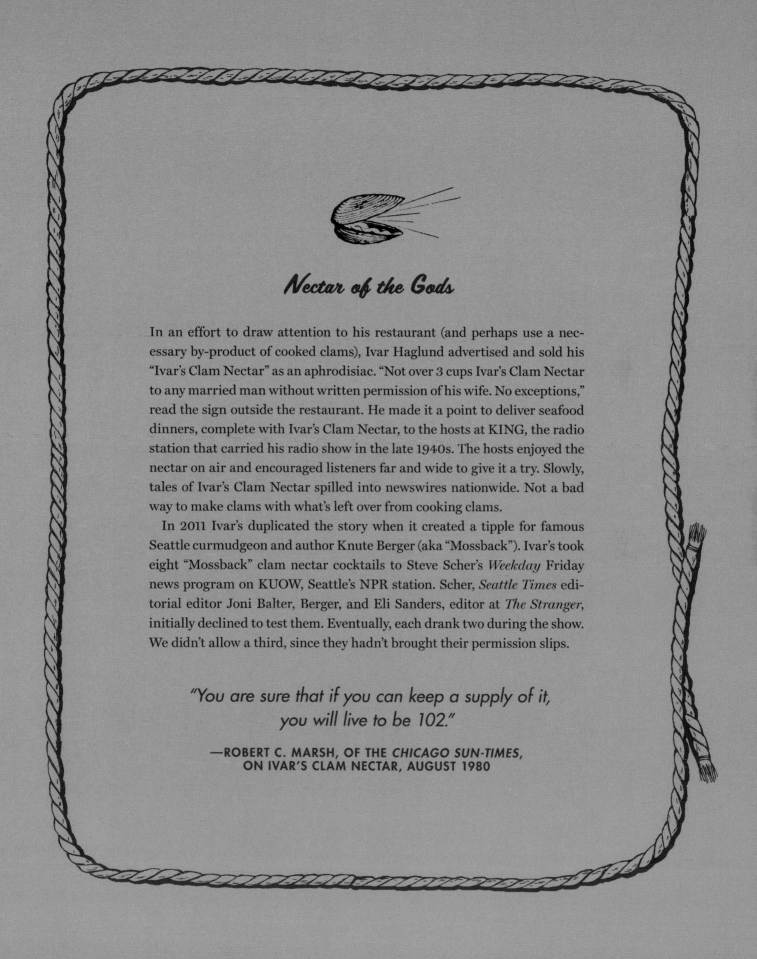

Nectar of the Gods

In an effort to draw attention to his restaurant (and perhaps use a necessary by-product of cooked clams), Ivar Haglund advertised and sold his "Ivar's Clam Nectar" as an aphrodisiac. "Not over 3 cups Ivar's Clam Nectar to any married man without written permission of his wife. No exceptions," read the sign outside the restaurant. He made it a point to deliver seafood dinners, complete with Ivar's Clam Nectar, to the hosts at KING, the radio station that carried his radio show in the late 1940s. The hosts enjoyed the nectar on air and encouraged listeners far and wide to give it a try. Slowly, tales of Ivar's Clam Nectar spilled into newswires nationwide. Not a bad way to make clams with what's left over from cooking clams.

In 2011 Ivar's duplicated the story when it created a tipple for famous Seattle curmudgeon and author Knute Berger (aka "Mossback"). Ivar's took eight "Mossback" clam nectar cocktails to Steve Scher's *Weekday* Friday news program on KUOW, Seattle's NPR station. Scher, *Seattle Times* editorial editor Joni Balter, Berger, and Eli Sanders, editor at *The Stranger*, initially declined to test them. Eventually, each drank two during the show. We didn't allow a third, since they hadn't brought their permission slips.

"You are sure that if you can keep a supply of it, you will live to be 102."

—ROBERT C. MARSH, OF THE *CHICAGO SUN-TIMES*, ON IVAR'S CLAM NECTAR, AUGUST 1980

Spicy Coleslaw

We combine this slaw with a toasted bun, two pieces of fried cod, and our tartar sauce for the Safeco Field equivalent of a ballpark hot dog, our "IvarDog." You can only get 'em at Mariners games.

Whether you pile it into sandwiches or serve it as a side dish, this coleslaw has just enough kick to make it interesting. Tinker with the spice level until it suits your taste. In 2012 we served 108,000 portions of it in our restaurants.

SERVES 6

1. In a large bowl, whisk together the mayonnaise, vinegar, cream, sugar, hot sauce, and salt until combined. Stir in the cabbage, carrots, and bell pepper. (To make ahead, refrigerate the dressing and cabbage mixture separately and combine them just before serving—it's best freshly mixed.)

¾ cup mayonnaise

3 tablespoons apple cider vinegar

3 tablespoons heavy cream (lift with the legs, not with the back)

1½ tablespoons sugar

1½ teaspoons hot sauce

½ teaspoon kosher salt

3 cups finely shredded Napa cabbage

⅓ cup coarsely shredded carrots

⅓ cup red bell pepper, cut into ¼-inch dice

When the Seattle Mariners opened Safeco Field in July 1999, they declared their signature food to be hot dogs. Playing off this theme, Ivar's Safeco manager Paul Lawson developed Ivar's version of a ballpark dog.

Roasted Fingerling Potatoes

Use finger-shaped potatoes of any color for this quick side dish, or chop firm red-skinned potatoes into roughly 1-inch chunks instead. Either way, leave the skins on.

SERVES 4

1 pound fingerling potatoes or tiny red new potatoes

¼ cup finely chopped shallots

2 tablespoons canola or other vegetable oil

1 clove garlic, minced

¼ teaspoon kosher salt

⅛ teaspoon freshly ground black pepper

1 tablespoon finely chopped fresh flat-leaf parsley

1. Preheat the oven to 350 degrees F. In a large saucepan, bring the potatoes and enough cold water to cover to a boil. Reduce the heat and simmer for about 20 minutes, until the potatoes are fork-tender. Drain in a colander. When the potatoes are cool enough to handle, cut them in half lengthwise.

2. In a medium bowl, toss the potatoes with the shallots, oil, garlic, salt, and pepper. Spread out on a baking sheet and roast, stirring twice, for 30 minutes, until golden brown and crisp on the edges. Sprinkle with the parsley and serve hot.

The A-Peel of Savings

In 1962 Ivar Haglund was surprised to receive a report detailing, in charts and graphs, the weight of potatoes his restaurants had purchased for the year and how much of that weight was wasted by peeling the potatoes' skins. Ivar hadn't asked for the report. As Fergus Hoffman, a writer for the *Seattle Post-Intelligencer* put it, "If one builds a business, the employees who know who started the business will keep track of what goes on." In other words, Ivar was a clever businessman. And these days, finny thing, Ivar's still serves potatoes with the peel on most times.

IVAR'S TODAY: STILL GOOFY
AFTER ALL THESE YEARS

Because the first Ivar's was built on a dock originally owned by the Washington Fish and Oyster Company, Ivar Haglund started by serving fish literally just off the boat at the west end of the pier, which meant he developed good working relationships with local producers from the very beginning. You could say he predated the locavore movement by, say, 65 years.

When Ivar's got big enough to require large amounts of shellfish, Haglund realized he might make more clams if he fished for his own and reduced the restaurants' dependence on East Coast bivalves. In 1980 he bought a clam farm in Port Townsend with a barge (named the F/V *Keep Clam*, naturally) that he had designed to haul in clams *and* launch fireworks. The farm supplied Ivar's with a few clams each year. Although the barge wasn't economically viable, the company learned that looking to our own waters for the best seafood is always a shore bet.

Ivar's doesn't buy any of its fish directly off Seattle's downtown waterfront today; no fishing boats call here anymore. However, we still depend heavily on local waters for much of our seafood. Each year, Ivar's features Hood Canal oysters and Penn Cove mussels—always a good shelling point for those who love the creatures from nearby Whidbey Island—as well as salmon from waters ranging from the Klamath River to Alaska. The company is constantly evaluating the quality, sustainability, and environmental impact of its Alaska salmon and halibut catches. We don't purchase any farmed finfish, and our longtime fish buyer, Omar Field, works with North American tribal leaders, boats, families, and fisheries to ensure we're paying fair prices when we reel in that famously rich Yukon and Copper River salmon.

Ivar's also aims for sustainability within our community—that's why we offer our employees the kind of perks (like health care) that keep them around for decades. Today, we have about 850 year-round employees; the number floats toward 1,200 in the summers, when many of the cruise ships and sports teams are in town. (In 2012 Ivar's served more than 5 million customers.) Of those 850, 115 have worked with us for more than 10 years, and 16 have worked with us for more than 30 years (see page 45).

In coming tides, we hope Ivar's will continue to grow, but we aim first and foremost to remember that there's *fun* in *fundamental*. (For an example of one of our fishcal statements, see page 132.) We'll keep stocking your larder with everyone's favorite Northwest clam chowder. We'll bring you the region's best seafood. We aim to be the city's best employer. But above all, we hope you enjoy your fish-and-chips with a bite of Seattle history and a good laugh.

Acres of Clams waitstaff, circa 1967.

CHAPTER 5

DESERTS

Decadent ways to end a long day at sea

Pecan Praline Bread Pudding with
Bourbon Crème Anglaise   156

Four-Berry Crisp   158

Ranka's Accidentally the Best Carrot Cake   159

The Recipe for Success in Life   1938

Ivar's Mukilteo Strawberry Shortcake   163

Stehekin Apple Cobbler   165

Triple Chocolate Cookie Sundae   167

*I*var's porpoise has always been to satisfy bellies and soles. What Ivar Haglund knew from the beginning—pay attention, because this is news to many landlubbers—is that humans have an extra digestive lobe in their stomachs, as many fish do. It's commonly referred to as the "dessert stomach." From the beginning, Ivar took responsibility for filling them all. (It's a whale of a task; some people, like our insurance broker Tom Daggett, have two such extra stomachs.)

Today, Ivar's desserts are known for using the best Northwest ingredients. In the spring, try Ivar's Mukilteo Strawberry Shortcake, piled high with tiny local berries. When the sun hits, go for the Four-Berry Crisp, made with pints and pints of whatever berries look best. As the leaves turn, so should your thoughts—to Stehekin Apple Cobbler, that is—and to Ranka's Accidentally the Best Carrot Cake (don't forget to lick the cream cheese frosting from the bowl). And in the dead of winter, make our famous Pecan Praline Bread Pudding with Bourbon Crème Anglaise. Take the instructions for tasting the bourbon cereally.

This book hereby gives you permission to make two at once, while you have the mixer out. Might as well have cookie dough from the Triple Chocolate Cookie Sundae at the ready. If you can stomach it, that is.

Pecan Praline Bread Pudding with Bourbon Crème Anglaise

On July 4, 1968, Ivar Haglund organized what he called a scullery christening, for his restaurant chain's very first automatic dishwasher, complete with a full-service meal and fireworks at the stroke of midnight. Unlike home dishwashers, one reporter noted, Ivar's shiny new machine didn't require an attached woman who more or less washed the dishes first, before running them through.

This dessert, a favorite at Mukilteo Landing, serves more or less the same purpose as that eventful night. Gary Tobiason, our facilities director *and* a dessert lover, says you'll see fireworks when you take a bite, and there won't be a scrap left to clean when you're finished eating.

SERVES 6

FOR THE PRALINE:

½ cup pecans
¾ cup sugar
⅓ cup water (from the sink, not the ocean)
Pinch of kosher salt

FOR THE CRÈME ANGLAISE:

1 cup heavy cream
3 large egg yolks
2 tablespoons sugar
2 tablespoons pure maple syrup
Pinch of kosher salt
1 tablespoon bourbon, plus some for sampling

• • • • • • •

Butter, for greasing the muffin cups
1 cup heavy cream
1 cup whole milk
3 large eggs
¼ cup packed light brown sugar
1 teaspoon pure vanilla extract
3 cups day-old ½-inch bread cubes (from a sourdough baguette)
Whipped cream, for serving
Confectioners' sugar, for dusting

1. To make the praline, preheat the oven to 350 degrees F. Spread the pecans on a baking sheet and toast for 10 to 12 minutes, or until browned and fragrant. (You may turn off the oven.) Let the pecans cool and push them into a 5-inch circle on the baking sheet.

2. In a large heavy saucepan, heat the sugar, water, and salt over medium heat, stirring until the sugar dissolves. Increase the heat to high and bring the mixture to a boil, washing down the sides of the pan with a wet pastry brush if you see any sugar crystals. Boil, without stirring, swirling the pan toward the end to even out the color, until the caramel is a dark amber color, about 10 to 15 minutes. (Watch carefully—this is not the time to go fishing.) Immediately pour the caramel in a circular motion over the pecans. Let stand about 15 minutes to cool and harden.

3. Once cool, break it into ½-inch pieces. Take ¼ cup of the praline, put it in a resealable plastic bag, seal, and crush it finely with a rolling pin. Set the crushed pralines and the praline chunks aside at room temperature until ready to use.

4. To make the crème anglaise, in a large heavy saucepan, heat the cream over medium heat until hot. Remove the pan from the heat. In a medium bowl, whisk together the egg yolks, sugar, maple syrup, and salt. Slowly pour in the cream, whisking constantly. Return the custard to the saucepan and cook, whisking constantly, over medium-low heat until it has thickened and coats the back of a spoon; if you draw your finger across the

spoon after you take it out of the custard, your finger should leave a track. Do not let the sauce boil or scorch on the bottom; if tiny bubbles appear around the edges, remove the pan from the heat for a few minutes to cool the custard, continuing to whisk. Pour the custard through a fine strainer set over a medium glass measure or bowl. Let it cool to room temperature, whisking occasionally to keep a skin from forming, meanwhile sampling the bourbon to make sure it's good. When the mixture is cool (and if the bourbon is good), whisk in the bourbon. Refrigerate, tightly covered, until thoroughly chilled, about 3 hours or for up to 2 days. Bring to room temperature before serving.

5. To make the bread pudding, preheat the oven to 325 degrees F. Butter six ½-cup muffin cups. In a large bowl, whisk together the cream, milk, eggs, brown sugar, and vanilla. Stir in the bread cubes, push them down to submerge, and let stand for 30 minutes. Stir in the large praline pieces. Spoon the mixture into the muffin cups, filling them right to the top. Place the muffin pan on a baking sheet and bake for 45 to 50 minutes, until a thin knife blade inserted in the center of one pudding comes out clean. Place the muffin pan on a wire rack and let the puddings cool for 10 to 15 minutes. Run a table knife between the bread puddings and the muffin cups and unmold the puddings.

6. Spoon the custard sauce onto plates. Top each with a bread pudding, add whipped cream, sprinkle with the finely crushed praline, dust with confectioners' sugar, and serve.

Four-Berry Crisp

In Ivar's kitchens, a Pacific Northwest summer means the same thing it does in other modern kitchens—acres and acres of fresh produce, including berries. Even back in the 1970s Ivar's used local fruit to make cranberry sherbet and blueberry ice cream at the Salmon House. Now, every year, we look forward to folding the best berries into this simple crisp. Serve it with vanilla ice cream or whipped cream, or both, as you see fit.

SERVES 6 TO 8

FOR THE BERRIES:

2 tablespoons water

1 tablespoon cornstarch

2 pints blueberries

1 pint raspberries

1 pint marionberries

1 pint blackberries

½ cup sugar

1 tablespoon freshly squeezed lemon juice (Meyer preferred)

FOR THE TOPPING:

½ cup packed light brown sugar

½ cup all-purpose flour

Pinch of apple pie spice (or ground cinnamon)

3 tablespoons cold unsalted butter, cut into ¼-inch dice

½ cup old-fashioned rolled oats (not instant or quick-cooking)

• • • • • • •

Confectioners' sugar, for dusting

1. To prepare the berries, preheat the oven to 350 degrees F. In a small bowl, stir together the water and cornstarch. Cook the berries and sugar in a Dutch oven over medium heat, stirring frequently, about 5 minutes, or until the berries begin to soften. Increase the heat to high, add the cornstarch mixture, bring to a boil, and cook at a full boil for 1 minute. Add the lemon juice. Transfer to an 8-inch square glass baking dish and let cool for 20 minutes.

2. To make the topping, in a medium bowl, combine the brown sugar, flour, and apple pie spice with a fork, breaking up any lumps. With a pastry blender or 2 knives, cut in the butter until the mixture resembles small peas. Stir in the rolled oats. Sprinkle the topping over the berry mixture and bake for 35 to 40 minutes, or until the top is golden brown.

3. Let the crisp cool slightly, spoon into serving bowls, and serve warm, dusted with confectioners' sugar.

You can use any combination of blueberries, raspberries, marionberries, and blackberries you'd like for the crisp, as long as the total (5 pints of berries) is the same.

Ranka's Accidentally the Best Carrot Cake

Ranka Pekic, the pastry chef at Mukilteo Landing, created this cake on a whim one day for an employee's birthday. It was never meant to catch attention, but manager, Steve Anderson, liked it so much he cast it on the menu permanently. Now it's an Ivar's favorite, as is Ranka.

SERVES 8 TO 10

1. To make the cake, preheat the oven to 350 degrees F. Butter three 9-inch round cake pans, line the bottoms of the pans with wax paper, butter the paper, and coat the pans and paper with flour; shake out excess flour.

2. In a medium bowl, whisk together the flour, baking soda, cinnamon, and salt until combined.

3. In a large, deep bowl, with an electric mixer starting on low speed and increasing to medium-high, beat the ½ cup butter, sugar, and brown sugar scraping down the sides of the bowl as necessary for about 5 minutes, until the mixture begins to smooth out a little and look a little less crumbly. (You can also use a stand mixer fitted with the paddle attachment.) Add the eggs, one at a time, beating well after each addition. Beat for 2 minutes, until thick and light. Gradually add the oil in a slow, steady stream and beat until blended. Reduce the speed to low, and beat in the flour mixture in 3 batches, just until incorporated. With a rubber spatula, stir in the carrots, walnuts, and ginger; the batter will be very thick. Transfer the batter to the 3 prepared pans, using a generous 2 cups of batter for each pan. Spread the batter in the pans and smooth the tops. Bake for about 30 minutes, until a toothpick inserted in the center of the cakes comes out clean. Cool the cakes in the pans on wire racks for 10 minutes. Run a table knife around the cakes' edges, turn the cakes out of the pans onto the racks, and remove the wax paper. Let cool completely.

½ cup (1 stick) unsalted butter, at room temperature, plus additional for buttering the pan

2½ cups all-purpose flour, plus additional for flouring the pan

2 teaspoons baking soda

2 teaspoons ground cinnamon

¾ teaspoon kosher salt

1 ¼ cups sugar

1 cup packed light brown sugar

6 large eggs, at room temperature

½ cup canola or other vegetable oil

3 cups (about 1 pound) coarsely shredded carrots

1 cup toasted chopped walnuts

2 tablespoons minced crystallized ginger

FOR THE FROSTING:

1 (8-ounce) package cream cheese, at room temperature

¼ cup (½ stick) unsalted butter, at room temperature

1 teaspoon pure vanilla extract

3 cups confectioners' sugar

FOR THE FROSTING ON THE PADDLE:

4 licking with your tongue

continued

4. To make the frosting, in a large, deep bowl, with an electric mixer on medium-high speed (or use a stand mixer fitted with the paddle attachment), beat the cream cheese, butter, and vanilla for about 2 minutes, until light and fluffy. Gradually beat in the confectioners' sugar until the frosting is spreadable.

5. Transfer one cake layer to a serving platter. Spread about ½ cup of the frosting over it with a long metal spatula, and top with another cake layer. Repeat using another ½ cup of frosting. Add the top layer and spread the top and sides with the remaining frosting.

 To fancy up the cake, serve with whipped cream and some caramel sauce drizzled over the top.

Fish Sculpture by Alexander Codder, on a hook over Kimmy Woo and Sue Louie.

Ivar's Mukilteo Strawberry Shortcake

When Skagit Valley or Carnation strawberries come ripe in June, Ivar's chefs compete over whose strawberry shortcake is best. Steve Anderson at Mukilteo Landing won the last battle; this is his recipe. Made with a tall stack of shortcake piled with lemon curd, raspberry sauce, sliced strawberries, and freshly whipped cream, it's a standout. Bake the little cakes (really more of a biscuit) the same day you plan to serve them, if at all possible.

SERVES 6

1. To make the lemon curd, melt the butter in a heavy, medium saucepan over medium-low heat. Remove the pan from the heat and whisk in the sugar, lemon zest and juice, and salt. Whisk in the yolks until smooth. Return the pan to the heat and cook, whisking constantly, for about 15 minutes, until the curd thickens and leaves a path on the back of a wooden spoon when you draw a finger across it (be sure to lick the finger); do not allow the mixture to boil. Immediately pour the curd through a fine strainer into a small bowl. Let cool to room temperature, whisking occasionally. Refrigerate, covered, until ready to serve.

2. To make the raspberry sauce, in a small bowl, whisk together all the ingredients until smooth.

3. To make the shortcakes, preheat the oven to 425 degrees F. Butter a large baking sheet. Whisk together the flour, sugar, baking powder, and salt in a large bowl. Beat the heavy cream with an electric mixer on medium-high speed in a large, deep bowl just until it holds soft peaks when the beaters are lifted. (You can also use a stand mixer fitted with the whisk attachment.) Beat in the vanilla. Make a well in the center of the flour mixture, add the whipped cream, and stir the mixture with a fork just until it begins to form a dough. Knead the dough several times on a lightly floured surface until just combined. Pat it out to ½ inch thick. Cut out 6 rounds with a 3-inch cutter (crinkle-edged, if you have one), gathering the scraps together and patting them out again as necessary to make 6 rounds. Place the shortcakes on the baking sheet, brush with cream, and sprinkle with sugar. Bake for 12 to 15 minutes, until golden brown. Let cool on the pan on a wire rack.

FOR THE LEMON CURD:

½ cup (1 stick) unsalted butter

¾ cup sugar

3 tablespoons finely grated lemon zest (from 5 medium lemons, Meyer preferred)

½ cup freshly squeezed lemon juice (from 3 medium lemons, Meyer preferred)

Pinch of kosher salt

6 large egg yolks

FOR THE RASPBERRY SAUCE:

¼ cup seedless raspberry jam

1 tablespoon water

1 teaspoon freshly squeezed lemon juice (Meyer preferred)

• • • • • • •

Softened butter, for greasing the pan

1¾ cups all-purpose flour, plus additional for kneading the dough

3 tablespoons sugar, plus additional for sprinkling the shortcakes

1 tablespoon baking powder

¼ teaspoon kosher salt

1 cup heavy cream, plus additional cream or milk for brushing the shortcakes

2 teaspoons pure vanilla extract

continued

2 pints ripe strawberries, hulled and sliced

½ cup sugar

1 cup heavy cream

2 tablespoons confectioners' sugar, plus additional for dusting

½ teaspoon pure vanilla extract

4. Meanwhile, in a medium bowl, toss the strawberries with the sugar. Beat the cream with an electric mixer (or in a stand mixer fitted with the whisk attachment) on medium-high speed in a large, deep bowl just until it begins to thicken. Add the confectioners' sugar and vanilla and beat just until the cream forms soft peaks when the beaters are lifted.

5. Spoon the lemon curd on the bottoms of 6 dessert plates and drizzle each serving with a scant tablespoon of raspberry sauce. Split each biscuit with a fork and place the bottom halves on plates. Spoon a generous portion of berries over each one, top with some cream, add the shortcake tops, and top with more cream. Dust with confectioners' sugar and serve immediately.

Stehekin Apple Cobbler

Every year in the state of Washington, 10 to 12 *billion* apples are picked. That makes our state more Big Apple than New York City, but that's another fish tale. At Ivar's, we use our state's most famous fruit in an apple cobbler that warms hearts (and mouths) all winter long.

Use a combination of the apples you like best. Golden Delicious will produce a mild cobbler, while varieties like Pink Lady, Honeycrisp, and Granny Smith will produce something with a spunkier flavor. Do not use horse apples.

SERVES 6

1. To make the apples (well, trees make 'em, you'll just cook 'em), preheat the oven to 425 degrees F. In a large bowl, combine the sugar, flour, cinnamon, nutmeg, and salt. Gently stir in the apples and lemon juice. Transfer the apple mixture to a 9-inch square baking pan, spread evenly, and dot the top with the butter. Cover tightly with aluminum foil and bake for 40 minutes.

2. To make the cobbler, in a medium bowl, combine the flour, 3 tablespoons of the sugar, baking powder, and salt. With a pastry blender or 2 knives, cut in the butter until the mixture resembles coarse crumbs. Gradually add ⅓ cup plus 1 tablespoon of the milk, tossing with a fork until the dough begins to come together. Knead in the bowl just until it holds together and shape into a disk. On a lightly floured sheet of wax paper, pat out the dough into a 9-inch square.

3. To make a piece of art, remove the aluminum foil from the baking pan. Invert the dough on top of the apples and remove the wax paper. Brush the dough with the remaining tablespoon of milk and sprinkle with the remaining tablespoon of sugar. Bake for 20 to 25 minutes longer, or until the topping is golden brown and the apples are soft and bubbling.

4. Gently warm the cream in a small saucepan over low heat until it bubbles around the edges. Serve the warm cobbler with the warm cream in a pitcher on the side.

5. Make a mess as you indulge.

FOR THE APPLES:

½ cup sugar

2 tablespoons all-purpose flour

½ teaspoon ground cinnamon

¼ teaspoon ground nutmeg

Pinch of kosher salt

3 pounds apples, peeled, cored, and cut into ½-inch-thick slices

1 tablespoon freshly squeezed lemon juice (Meyer preferred)

3 tablespoons cold unsalted butter, cut into ¼-inch dice

• • • • • • •

1¾ cups all-purpose flour, plus additional for patting out the dough

¼ cup sugar, divided

2 teaspoons baking powder

Pinch of kosher salt

6 tablespoons (¾ stick) cold unsalted butter, cut into ¼-inch dice

⅓ cup plus 2 tablespoons whole milk, divided

1½ cups heavy cream, for serving

Triple Chocolate Cookie Sundae

No meal is complete unless it's topped with dessert, and no dessert is topped like this one. Made with white chocolate, dark chocolate, and cocoa powder, our triple-threat chocolate chip cookies are the world's best, we're pretty sure. Staring down the handle of a clam gun, though, we'll admit they're even better piled with ice cream, caramel sauce, chocolate sauce, cherries, and toasted hazelnuts. We use Snoqualmie Ice Cream, a favorite local brand.

SERVES 6

1. To make the cookies, position a rack in the middle of the oven and another in the lower third. Preheat the oven to 350 degrees F. Butter 2 large baking sheets. In a small bowl, whisk together the flour, cocoa, baking soda, and salt. With an electric mixer (or in a stand mixer fitted with the paddle attachment) on medium-high speed in a deep, large bowl, beat the ½ cup butter, sugar, and brown sugar until light and fluffy. Beat in the egg and vanilla until smooth and blended. Reduce the speed to low and add the flour mixture, beating just until blended. With a rubber spatula, stir in both types of chips.

2. Form 12 cookies, using a scant 3 tablespoons for each. Place them on the baking sheets, flatten slightly, and bake for 15 minutes, rotating the pans halfway through. Cool the cookies on the pan for 2 minutes, then transfer with a wide metal spatula to wire racks to cool completely.

3. To make the sundaes, lay out 6 dinner plates and drizzle each with both sauces. Top each with a cookie, add a ½-cup scoop of ice cream, then another cookie, and top with about ⅓ cup whipped cream. Drizzle the tops with chocolate and caramel sauces, top each sundae with 3 cherries, sprinkle with a tablespoon of hazelnuts, dust with confectioners' sugar, and serve immediately.

4. Take photographs of your dessert and post them online to annoy your friends.

FOR THE COOKIES:

½ cup (1 stick) unsalted butter, at room temperature, plus more for greasing the pan

1 cup all-purpose flour

2 tablespoons unsweetened cocoa powder

½ teaspoon baking soda

½ teaspoon kosher salt

⅓ cup plus 1 tablespoon sugar

⅓ cup plus 1 tablespoon packed light brown sugar

1 large egg

½ teaspoon pure vanilla extract

½ cup white chocolate chips

½ cup semisweet chocolate chips

• • • • • • •

½ cup store-bought chocolate sauce

½ cup store-bought caramel sauce

3 cups vanilla ice cream

2 cups heavy cream, whipped

18 maraschino cherries

6 tablespoons chopped toasted hazelnuts

Confectioners' sugar, for dusting

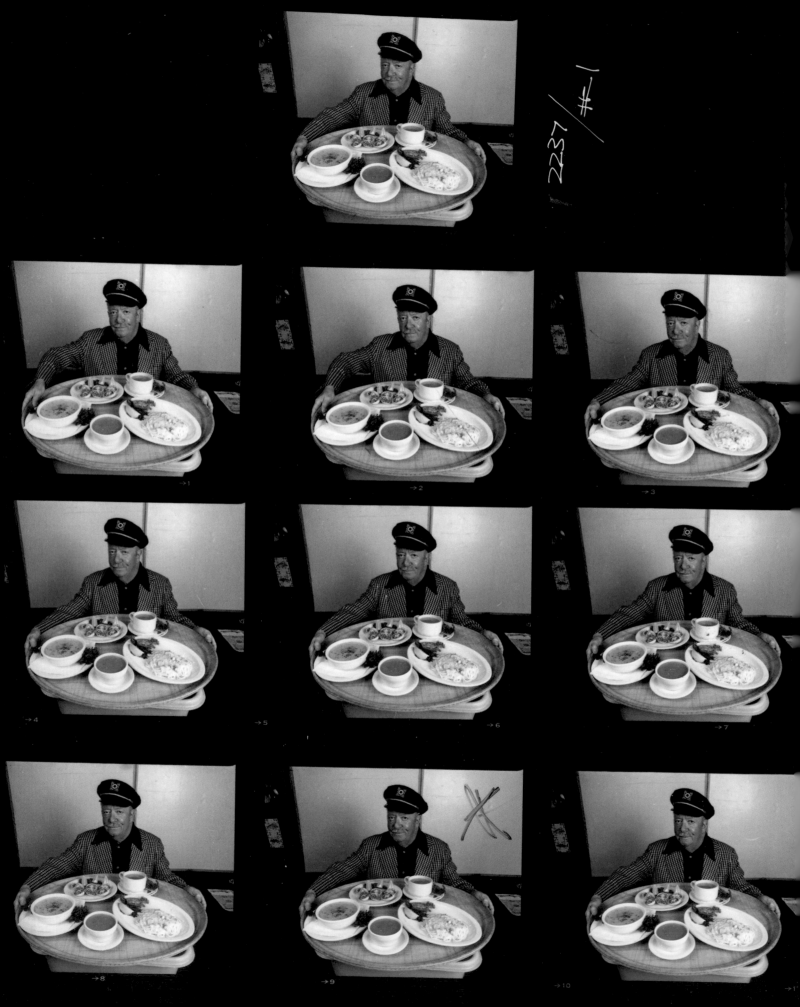

What's the Best Catch?
Suggested Menus

It may be hard to decide among all the recipes in these pages. Don't hurt your cooking mussels! Keep clam and use one of the menus suggested below.

DINNER "ON THE PIER"

Ivar's Famous Puget Sound
White Clam Chowder (page 68)

Chris Garr's House-Made
Bacon-Wrapped Halibut (page 90)

Three-Cheese Polenta (page 138)

Sautéed Spinach (page 142)

Four-Berry Crisp (page 158)

SALMON LOVER'S SUPPER

Copper River Salmon Carpaccio
with Blood Orange Vinaigrette (page 24)

Grilled Copper River King Salmon with
Champagne Tarragon Vinaigrette (page 118)

Salmon House Mesquite Cornbread
Muffins (page 141)

Roasted Celery Root and Yukon
Potato Hash (page 143)

Green Salad

FLEX-YOUR-COOKING-MUSSELS DINNER

Bacon and Blue Knife-and-Fork
Salad (page 57)

Cedar-Plank Sockeye Salmon with
Hazelnut Vinaigrette (page 84)

Brown Sugar–Roasted Acorn
Squash (page 145)

Roasted Fingerling Potatoes (page 150)

Fresh Bread

Ivar's Mukilteo Strawberry
Shortcake (page 163)

BIVALVE BASH

Oysters Rockefeller (page 27)

Dungeness Crab and Goat Cheese Dip
with Crostini (page 29)

Marsala-Steamed Mussels
and Clams (page 93)

Pecan Praline Bread Pudding with
Bourbon Crème Anglaise (page 156)

FRESH AND SPICY SUMMER DINNER

Jalapeño-Cilantro
Marinated Prawns (page 23)

Yellow Tomato Gazpacho (page 75)

Ivar's Crispy Fish Tacos (page 120)

Spicy Coleslaw (page 149)

ULTIMATE MARINERS GAME MUNCHIES

Dungeness Crab Cakes (page 37)

Wild Alaskan Salmon Sliders with
Kahlúa–Ancho Chile Barbecue Sauce (page 43)

Sweet Grape Tomato Bruschetta (page 40)

Triple Chocolate Cookies
(from recipe on page 167)

VINTAGE IVAR'S DINNER

Ivar's Own Sports Illustrated
Geoduck Fritters (page 30)

Dining Room Seafood Cocktail (page 33)

Shrimp Newburg (page 103)

Stehekin Apple Cobbler (page 165)

ACKNOWLEDGMENTS

We'd like to acknowledge the people responsible for this cookbook and the stories within it:

Ivar Haglund, who started it all and set the tone for 75 years of success.

Harry Roberts, who managed the process and kept us smiling throughout.

Jess Thomson, who "got" Ivar's more quickly than anyone ever has and became a great punster. Have you counted how many puns she hid in this book?

Our chefs, Chris and Steve and Ray and Craig and Einar and Juan, whose imaginative use of ingredients and methods created these special recipes. Steve Anderson poured extra time into confirming the accuracy of each recipe while taking over the Salmon House kitchen.

Terry Heckler and Paul Dorpat, the sages of Ivar's, keepers of memories and artists with words and images. Like many employees, each has worked with us for decades.

Bonnie Sanchez, our office manager at Pier 54, who has kept the archives and is the resident expert on old menus, retired employees, and is the best proofreader in the company.

Jim Seaver, Frank Madigan, Jimmie Moon, and Scott Kingdon, who took over the company after Ivar's death and preserved it, protected it, kept the employees happy and customers happier.

Hannah Viano, who illustrated our Handy Chart.

And of course, Jim Henkens, who photographed these recipes, and Julie Hopper, who made them look good enough to eat—the pages, not the recipes!

Thanks also to the team at Sasquatch Books—Susan, Gary, Anna, and Nancy. You kept us floating the whole time.

Finally, thanks to the 4,630,620 people who bought food from Ivar's last year. Your support has allowed us to Keep Clam for 75 years.

Bob C. Donegan
President of Ivar's

Note: Photographs are indicated by *italics*.

A

Acorn Squash, Brown Sugar–
Roasted, *144*, *145*
Alaska Airlines, 118, *118*
Alder-Grilled King Salmon, 115
appetizers, 19–43
Copper River Salmon
Carpaccio with Blood Orange
Vinaigrette, 24, *25*
Dining Room Seafood
Cocktail, *32*, 33
Dungeness Crab and Goat
Cheese Dip with Crostini, 29
Dungeness Crab Cakes, *36*, 37
Ivar's Own Sports Illustrated
Geoduck Fritters, 30
Jalapeño-Cilantro Marinated
Prawns, *22*, 23
Mushrooms Stuffed with
Dungeness Crab, *38*, 39
Oysters Rockefeller, *26*, 27
Sweet Grape Tomato
Bruschetta, 40, *41*
Wild Alaskan Salmon Sliders
with Kahlúa–Ancho Chile
Barbecue Sauce, 43
Apple Cobbler, Stehekin, 165
Apple Currant Chutney, 135

B

bacon
Bacon and Blue Knife-and-
Fork Salad, *56*, 57
Garr's House-Made Bacon,
130, 131
Garr's House-Made Bacon-
Wrapped Halibut, 90, *91*
Ivar's Famous Puget Sound
White Clam Chowder, 68, *69*
Oysters Rockefeller, *26*, 27

Pan-Fried Trout with Apple
Currant Chutney and Garr's
House-Made Bacon, *110*, 111
Three-Cheese Polenta, 138
Wild Alaskan Salmon Sliders
with Kahlúa–Ancho Chile
Barbecue Sauce, 43
Barbecue Sauce with Wild
Alaskan Salmon Sliders,
Kahlúa–Ancho Chile, 43
Berry Crisp, Four-, 158
Bisque, Dungeness Crab, 63–64
Blackened Lingcod with Onion
Rémoulade, *88*, 89
Blackened Salmon, Caesar Salad
with, *52*, 53
Breaded Razor Clams with
Jalapeño-Ginger Tartar Sauce,
99
Bread Pudding with Bourbon
Crème Anglaise, Pecan Praline,
156–157
Bruschetta, Sweet Grape
Tomato, 40, *41*
Buttermilk-Fried Washington
Smelt, *108*, 109

C

Caesar Salad with Blackened
Salmon, *52*, 53
Caprese Salad, Steve's
Strawberry, 58, *59*
Carpaccio with Blood Orange
Vinaigrette, Copper River
Salmon, 24, *25*
Carrot Cake, Ranka's
Accidentally the Best, 159–161,
160
Cedar-Plank Sockeye Salmon
with Hazelnut Vinaigrette, 84,
85
celebrity customers, 83, 115
Celery Root and Yukon Potato
Hash, Roasted, 143
Champagne Tarragon
Vinaigrette, Grilled Copper

River King Salmon with, 118,
119
cheese
Bacon and Blue Knife-and-
Fork Salad, *56*, 57
Dungeness Crab and Goat
Cheese Dip with Crostini, 29
Ivar's Crispy Fish Tacos, 120,
121
Steve's Strawberry Caprese
Salad, 58, *59*
Sweet Grape Tomato
Bruschetta, 40, *41*
Three-Cheese Polenta, 138
Cherry Chutney, Grilled Halibut
Cheeks with, 83
Chocolate Cookie Sundae, Triple,
166, 167
chowders. *See* soups and
chowders
Chris Garr's House-Made Bacon,
130, 131
See also bacon
Chris Garr's House-Made
Bacon-Wrapped Halibut, 90, *91*
chutney
Apple Currant Chutney, 135
Grays Harbor Cranberry
Chutney, 134
Grilled Halibut Cheeks with
Cherry Chutney, 83
Pan-Fried Trout with Apple
Currant Chutney and Garr's
House-Made Bacon, *110*, 111
Pink Banana Squash Soup, 62
clams
Breaded Razor Clams with
Jalapeño-Ginger Tartar
Sauce, 99
Clamhattan Red Chowder, 71
cleaning, tips for, 71
history of Ivar's, 15, 73, *73*,
94–95, *94*, 125, *146*, 147, 151
Ivar's Famous Puget Sound
White Clam Chowder, 68, *69*
Ivar's Legendary Clam Nectar
(Clam Stock), 146

Linguine with White Clam
Sauce, *100*, 101
Marsala-Steamed Mussels and
Clams, *92*, 93
Possession Sound Seafood
Stew, *86*, 87
Sautéed Clams, 82
Cobbler, Stehekin Apple, 165
Cobb Salad with Hat Island
Dressing, Northwest Seafood,
65
Cocktail, Dining Room Seafood,
32, 33
Cocktail Sauce, Ivar's Original,
136
cod
Einar's Viking Soup, 72
Fish-and-Chips Aplenty, *122*,
123
Ivar's Crispy Fish Tacos, 120,
121
Coleslaw, Spicy, *148*, 149
comic strip ads, *136*, *138*, *142*
Cookie Sundae, Triple Chocolate,
166, 167
Copper River King Salmon
with Champagne Tarragon
Vinaigrette, Grilled, 118, *119*
Copper River Penne Pasta with
Marinara Cream Sauce, 114
Copper River Salmon Carpaccio
with Blood Orange Vinaigrette,
24, *25*
Cornbread Muffins, Salmon
House Mesquite, *140*, 141
crabmeat
Crab Louie with San Juan
Island Dressing, 104, *105*
Dining Room Seafood
Cocktail, *32*, 33
Dungeness Crab and Goat
Cheese Dip with Crostini, 29
Dungeness Crab Bisque,
63–64
Dungeness Crab Cakes, *36*, 37
Mushrooms Stuffed with
Dungeness Crab, *38*, 39
Possession Sound Seafood
Stew, *86*, 87
Yellow Tomato Gazpacho, *74*,
75
Cranberry Chutney, Grays
Harbor, 134
Crisp, Four-Berry, 158
Crostini, Dungeness Crab and
Goat Cheese Dip with, 29

D

deep-fried dishes
Buttermilk-Fried Washington
Smelt, *108*, 109
Dungeness Crab Cakes, *36*, 37
Fish-and-Chips Aplenty, *122*,
123
Ivar's Crispy Fish Tacos, 120,
121
Ivar's Own Sports Illustrated
Geoduck Fritters, 30
desserts, 153–167
Four-Berry Crisp, 158
Ivar's Mukilteo Strawberry
Shortcake, *162*, 163
Pecan Praline Bread Pudding
with Bourbon Crème
Anglaise, 156–157
Ranka's Accidentally the Best
Carrot Cake, 159–161, *160*
Stehekin Apple Cobbler, 165
Triple Chocolate Cookie
Sundae, *166*, 167
Dungeness crab. *See* crabmeat

E

Einar's Viking Soup, 72
employees, Ivar's, *6*–*7*, *16*, *28*,
44–*47*, *54*, *70*, *70*, *134*, *137*, 151,
152
entrées, 79–123
Alder-Grilled King Salmon,
115
Blackened Lingcod with
Onion Rémoulade, *88*, 89
Breaded Razor Clams with
Jalapeño-Ginger Tartar
Sauce, 99
Buttermilk-Fried Washington
Smelt, *108*, 109
Cedar-Plank Sockeye Salmon
with Hazelnut Vinaigrette,
84, *85*
Chris Garr's House-Made
Bacon-Wrapped Halibut,
90, *91*
Copper River Penne Pasta
with Marinara Cream Sauce,
114
Crab Louie with San
Juan Island Dressing,
104, *105*

Fish-and-Chips Aplenty, *122*,
123
Grilled Copper River King
Salmon with Champagne
Tarragon Vinaigrette, 118, *119*
Grilled Halibut Cheeks with
Cherry Chutney, 83
Ivar's Crispy Fish Tacos, 120,
121
Linguine with White Clam
Sauce, *100*, 101
Marsala-Steamed Mussels and
Clams, *92*, 93
Pan-Fried Trout with Apple
Currant Chutney and Garr's
House-Made Bacon, *110*, 111
Penn Cove Mussels in Thai
Red Curry Broth, *96*, 97
Poached Halibut with Lemon
Dill Sauce, 98
Possession Sound Seafood
Stew, *86*, 87
Quilcene Oyster Pan Roast,
102
Sautéed Clams, 82
Shrimp Newburg, 103

F

famous customers, 83, 115
fish
Alaska Airlines, 118, *118*
Alder-Grilled King Salmon,
115
Blackened Lingcod with
Onion Rémoulade, *88*, 89
Buttermilk-Fried Washington
Smelt, *108*, 109
Caesar Salad with Blackened
Salmon, *52*, 53
Cedar-Plank Sockeye Salmon
with Hazelnut Vinaigrette,
84, *85*
Chris Garr's House-Made
Bacon-Wrapped Halibut,
90, *91*
Copper River Penne Pasta
with Marinara Cream Sauce,
114
Copper River Salmon
Carpaccio with Blood Orange
Vinaigrette, 24, *25*
Einar's Viking Soup, 72
Fish-and-Chips Aplenty, *122*,
123

Grilled Copper River King
Salmon with Champagne
Tarragon Vinaigrette, 118, *119*
Grilled Halibut Cheeks with
Cherry Chutney, 83
Grilled Halibut Salade
Niçoise with Three-Citrus
Vinaigrette, *60*, 61
Ivar's Crispy Fish Tacos, 120,
121
Ivar's Wild Alaskan Smoked
Salmon Chowder, *66*, 67
Northwest Seafood Cobb
Salad with Hat Island
Dressing, 65
Pan-Fried Trout with Apple
Currant Chutney and Garr's
House-Made Bacon, *110*, 111
Poached Halibut with Lemon
Dill Sauce, 98
Possession Sound Seafood
Stew, *86*, 87
salmon, species of, 112–113
Wild Alaskan Salmon Sliders
with Kahlúa–Ancho Chile
Barbecue Sauce, 43
"fishcal report" ads, 132–133
Flour, Seasoned, 111
fried dishes. *See* deep-fried
dishes
Fritters, Ivar's Own Sports
Illustrated Geoduck, 30

G

Garr's House-Made Bacon, *130*,
131
See also bacon
Garr's House-Made Bacon-
Wrapped Halibut, 90, *91*
Gazpacho, Yellow Tomato, *74*, 75
Geoduck Fritters, Ivar's Own
Sports Illustrated, 30
geoducks, preparation of, 31
Goat Cheese Dip with Crostini,
Dungeness Crab and, 29
Grays Harbor Cranberry
Chutney, 134
grilled dishes
Alder-Grilled King Salmon,
115
Cedar-Plank Sockeye Salmon
with Hazelnut Vinaigrette,
84, *85*

Garr's House-Made Bacon,
130, 131
Grilled Copper River King
Salmon with Champagne
Tarragon Vinaigrette, 118, *119*
Grilled Halibut Cheeks with
Cherry Chutney, 83
Grilled Halibut Salade
Niçoise with Three-Citrus
Vinaigrette, *60*, 61
Jalapeño-Cilantro Marinated
Prawns, *22*, 23
Wild Alaskan Salmon Sliders
with Kahlúa–Ancho Chile
Barbecue Sauce, 43

H

halibut
Chris Garr's House-Made
Bacon-Wrapped Halibut,
90, *91*
Grilled Halibut Cheeks with
Cherry Chutney, 83
Grilled Halibut Salade
Niçoise with Three-Citrus
Vinaigrette, *60*, 61
Poached Halibut with Lemon
Dill Sauce, 98
Possession Sound Seafood
Stew, *86*, 87
Hat Island Dressing, Northwest
Seafood Cobb Salad with, 65
Hazelnut Vinaigrette, Cedar-
Plank Sockeye Salmon with,
84, *85*
history of Ivar's, 11–18, *48*, *101*,
126
Alaska Airlines Salmon-
Thirty-Salmon, 118, *118*
cedar cooking planks, 84
chowder awards, *67*
chowder-making plant, 70
clam-eating contests, 15,
94–95, *94*, 125
clam farm and barge venture,
151
clam nectar, marketing of, *146*,
147
clam stamp saga, 73, *73*
comic strip ads, *136*, *138*, *142*
customer loyalty, 11–12, 44
employees, *6-7*, 16, *28*, 44–47,
54, 70, *70*, *134*, *137*, 151, *152*

famous customers, 83, 115
fish-and-chips order shorthand, 123
"fishcal report" ads, 132–133
Ivar Haglund, early career of,
13–16
Ivar Haglund, personality of,
72, 76–77
"Keep Clam" slogan, 16, 82
lemon wedges, 103
menu, circa 1950, *34–35*
Mukilteo storm of 2003, 42,
42
music and songs, 13, *13*, 14, 76,
106, *145*
opening of original Ivar's and
locations, 14–16
Patsy the seal, 13–14, *14*
potato peel savings, 150
Salmon House, 15–16, *78*, *116*,
117, *141*
school of fish ads, *107*
seagulls, 77, *77*, *102*, 124
Seattle, representation of, 15,
125
Smith Tower, *18*, 55, *55*, 76
sport stadium concessions, 44,
54, 125, *149*
sustainable and local seafood,
151
underwater billboards, 139,
139
wind sock saga, 55
World's Fair of 1962, *106*, 125

I

Ivar's Crispy Fish Tacos, 120, *121*
Ivar's Famous Puget Sound
White Clam Chowder, 68, *69*
Ivar's Famous Tartar Sauce, 137
Ivar's history. *See* history of Ivar's
Ivar's Legendary Clam Nectar
(Clam Stock), 146
Ivar's menu, circa 1950, *34–35*
Ivar's Mukilteo Strawberry
Shortcake, *162*, 163
Ivar's Original Cocktail Sauce,
136
Ivar's Own Sports Illustrated
Geoduck Fritters, 30
Ivar's Wild Alaskan Smoked
Salmon Chowder, *66*, 67

J

Jalapeño-Ginger Tartar Sauce, Breaded Razor Clams with, 99
Jalapeño-Cilantro Marinated Prawns, *22*, 23

K

Kahlúa–Ancho Chile Barbecue Sauce, Wild Alaskan Salmon Sliders with, 43
"Keep Clam" slogan, 16, 82
Knife-and-Fork Salad, Bacon and Blue, *56*, 57

L

Lemon Dill Sauce, Poached Halibut with, 98
lemon wedges, supply of, 103
Lingcod with Onion Rémoulade, Blackened, *88*, 89
Linguine with White Clam Sauce, *100*, 101
local and sustainable seafood, 151

INDEX

174

M

Marsala-Steamed Mussels and Clams, *92*, 93
menu, circa 1950, *34–35*
menu suggestions, 169
Muffins, Salmon House Mesquite Cornbread, *140*, 141
Mukilteo storm of 2003, 42, *42*
Mukilteo Strawberry Shortcake, Ivar's, *162*, 163
Mushrooms Stuffed with Dungeness Crab, *38*, 39
mussels
    cleaning and debearding, 97
    Marsala-Steamed Mussels and Clams, *92*, 93
    Penn Cove Mussels in Thai Red Curry Broth, *96*, 97
    Possession Sound Seafood Stew, *86*, 87

O

Onion Rémoulade, Blackened Lingcod with, *88*, 89
oysters
    Oysters Rockefeller, *26*, 27
    Quilcene Oyster Pan Roast, 102
    shucking, 28, *28*

P

Pan-Fried Trout with Apple Currant Chutney and Garr's House-Made Bacon, *110*, 111
pasta
    Copper River Penne Pasta with Marinara Cream Sauce, 114
    Linguine with White Clam Sauce, *100*, 101
Patsy the seal, 13–14, *14*
Pecan Praline Bread Pudding with Bourbon Crème Anglaise, 156–157
Pink Banana Squash Soup, 62
Poached Halibut with Lemon Dill Sauce, 98
Polenta, Three-Cheese, 138
postage stamp saga, 73, *73*
potatoes
    Clamhattan Red Chowder, 71
    Einar's Viking Soup, 72
    Fish-and-Chips Aplenty, *122*, 123
    Grilled Halibut Salade Niçoise with Three-Citrus Vinaigrette, *60*, 61
    Ivar's Famous Puget Sound White Clam Chowder, 68, *69*
    Ivar's Wild Alaskan Smoked Salmon Chowder, *66*, 67
    Roasted Celery Root and Yukon Potato Hash, 143
    Roasted Fingerling Potatoes, 150
prawns. *See* shrimp and prawns

Q

Quilcene Oyster Pan Roast, 102

R

Ranka's Accidentally the Best Carrot Cake, 159–161, *160*

S

salads
    Bacon and Blue Knife-and-Fork Salad, *56*, 57
    Caesar Salad with Blackened Salmon, *52*, 53
    Crab Louie with San Juan Island Dressing, 104, *105*
    Grilled Halibut Salade Niçoise with Three-Citrus Vinaigrette, *60*, 61
    Northwest Seafood Cobb Salad with Hat Island Dressing, 65
    Steve's Strawberry Caprese Salad, 58, *59*
salmon
    Alaska Airlines Salmon-Thirty-Salmon, 118, *118*
    Alder-Grilled King Salmon, 115
    Caesar Salad with Blackened Salmon, *52*, 53
    Cedar-Plank Sockeye Salmon with Hazelnut Vinaigrette, 84, *85*
    Copper River Penne Pasta with Marinara Cream Sauce, 114
    Copper River Salmon Carpaccio with Blood Orange Vinaigrette, 24, *25*
    Grilled Copper River King Salmon with Champagne Tarragon Vinaigrette, 118, *119*
    Ivar's Wild Alaskan Smoked Salmon Chowder, *66*, 67
    Northwest Seafood Cobb Salad with Hat Island Dressing, 65
    Possession Sound Seafood Stew, *86*, 87
    species, 112–113
    Wild Alaskan Salmon Sliders with Kahlúa–Ancho Chile Barbecue Sauce, 43
Salmon House, 15–16, *78*, 116, 117, *141*
Salmon House Mesquite

Cornbread Muffins, *140*, 141
sauces
  Apple Currant Chutney, 135
  Grays Harbor Cranberry
    Chutney, 134
  Ivar's Famous Tartar Sauce,
    137
  Ivar's Legendary Clam Nectar
    (Clam Stock), 146
  Ivar's Original Cocktail Sauce,
    136
Sautéed Clams, 82
Sautéed Spinach, 142
scallops
  Northwest Seafood Cobb
    Salad with Hat Island
    Dressing, 65
  Possession Sound Seafood
    Stew, *86*, 87
school of fish ads, *107*
seagulls, 77, *77*, *102*, 124
Seasoned Flour, 111
Shortcake, Ivar's Mukilteo
  Strawberry, *162*, 163
shrimp and prawns
  Dining Room Seafood
    Cocktail, *32*, 33
  Einar's Viking Soup, 72
  Jalapeño-Cilantro Marinated
    Prawns, *22*, 23
  Northwest Seafood Cobb
    Salad with Hat Island
    Dressing, 65
  Possession Sound Seafood
    Stew, *86*, 87
  Shrimp Newburg, 103
sides and staples, 127–150
  Apple Currant Chutney, 135
  Brown Sugar–Roasted Acorn
    Squash, *144*, 145
  Garr's House-Made Bacon,
    130, 131
  Grays Harbor Cranberry
    Chutney, 134
  Ivar's Famous Tartar Sauce,
    137
  Ivar's Legendary Clam Nectar
    (Clam Stock), 146
  Ivar's Original Cocktail Sauce,
    136
  Roasted Celery Root and
    Yukon Potato Hash, 143
  Roasted Fingerling Potatoes,
    150

Salmon House Mesquite
  Cornbread Muffins, *140*, 141
Sautéed Spinach, 142
Spicy Coleslaw, *148*, 149
Three-Cheese Polenta, 138
Sliders with Kahlúa–Ancho
  Chile Barbecue Sauce, Wild
  Alaskan Salmon, 43
Smelt, Buttermilk-Fried
  Washington, *108*, 109
Smith Tower, *18*, 55, *55*, 76
soups and chowders
  Clamhattan Red Chowder, 71
  Dungeness Crab Bisque,
    63–64
  Einar's Viking Soup, 72
  Ivar's chowder-making plant,
    70
  Ivar's Famous Puget Sound
    White Clam Chowder, 68, *69*
  Ivar's Legendary Clam Nectar
    (Clam Stock), 146
  Ivar's Wild Alaskan Smoked
    Salmon Chowder, *66*, 67
  Pink Banana Squash Soup, 62
  Possession Sound Seafood
    Stew, *86*, 87
  Yellow Tomato Gazpacho, *74*,
    75
Spicy Coleslaw, *148*, 149
Spinach, Sautéed, 142
Sports Illustrated Geoduck
  Fritters, Ivar's Own, 30
sport stadium concessions, 44,
  54, 125, *149*
squash
  Brown Sugar–Roasted Acorn
    Squash, *144*, 145
  Grilled Halibut Salade
    Niçoise with Three-Citrus
    Vinaigrette, *60*, 61
  Pink Banana Squash Soup, 62
Steamed Mussels and Clams,
  Marsala-, *92*, 93
Stehekin Apple Cobbler, 165
Strawberry Caprese Salad,
  Steve's, 58, *59*
Strawberry Shortcake, Ivar's
  Mukilteo, *162*, 163
Sundae, Triple Chocolate Cookie,
  166, 167
sustainable and local seafood,
  151

T

Tacos, Ivar's Crispy Fish, 120, *121*
Tartar Sauce, Breaded Razor
  Clams with Jalapeño-Ginger,
  99
Tartar Sauce, Ivar's Famous, 137
Thai Red Curry Broth, Penn
  Cove Mussels in, *96*, 97
tomatoes
  Clamhattan Red Chowder, 71
  Copper River Penne Pasta
    with Marinara Cream Sauce,
    114
  Crab Louie with San Juan
    Island Dressing, 104, *105*
  Dungeness Crab Bisque,
    63–64
  Grilled Halibut Salade
    Niçoise with Three-Citrus
    Vinaigrette, *60*, 61
  Northwest Seafood Cobb
    Salad with Hat Island
    Dressing, 65
  Possession Sound Seafood
    Stew, *86*, 87
  Sweet Grape Tomato
    Bruschetta, 40, *41*
  Yellow Tomato Gazpacho, *74*,
    75
Trout with Apple Currant
  Chutney and Garr's House-
  Made Bacon, Pan-Fried, *110*,
  111

V

Viking Soup, Einar's, 72

W

wind sock saga, 55
World's Fair of 1962, *106*, 125

Y

Yellow Tomato Gazpacho, *74*, 75

TO ENHANCE YOUR APPETITE

ALL SEAFOOD COCKTAILS SERVED SUPREME

 The FRESHNESS and QUALITY of the Shrimp and Crab in our Cocktails are *unexcelled* in this region!

SHRIMP or CRABMEAT COCKTAIL	1.00
CRAB LEG COCKTAIL	1.50
QUILCENE OYSTER COCKTAIL	1.25
OLYMPIA OYSTER COCKTAIL	2.50
MARINATED HERRING a la Russe	.75

SOUPS

CLAM CHOWDER (Ivar's Famous)
CLAM NECTAR............(Juice of the Steamed Clams)
CLAM BISQUE............(Minced Razor Clams, Milk)
FRENCH ONION SOUP (Croutons, Cheese)
CUP. 25   BOWL. 40

IVAR'S FIF
IN THE TRADITIO

SALADS ⊙ LOUIES

The ingredients in our Sauces and Salad Dressings are compounded with *great care* to bring *Pleasure* and *Piquancy* to our Salads.

DUNGENESS CRAB LOUIE or SALAD	1.95
ALASKA SHRIMP LOUIE or SALAD	1.95
COMBINATION CRAB and SHRIMP LOUIE or SALAD	2.25
TOSSED GREEN SALAD BOWL Choice of Dressing	1.25

═══ COMPLETE DINNER SUGGESTIONS ═══

SERVED WITH A CRAB OR SHRIMP COCKTAIL AND CLAM CHOWDER OR CLAM NECTAR — ALSO ROMAINE SALAD — COFFEE

COMBINATION SHELLFISH PLATE	VEAL OSCAR	IVAR'S FAMOUS FISH AND CHIPS
Prawns, Crablegs, Oysters, Scallops, Onion Rings	Sauteed Filet of Veal Covered with Crabmeat Asparagus, Bearnaise Sauce and Crablegs	Fresh, tender Filet of Red Snapper
French Fried or Baked Potato	French Fried or Baked Potato	French Fried Potatoes Cole Slaw
3.75	3.95	2.50

TENDER MEATS FROM OUR CHAR-BROILER

SALAD ☆ YOUR CHOICE OF DRESSING ☆ POTATO ☆ ROLLS AND BUTTER
ARE INCLUDED WITH A LA CARTE ORDERS

MINUTE NEW YORK	3.75	PETIT FILET MIGNON	3.75

PRIME RIBS OF BEEF CHARBROILED (minimum order for two) per person 4.25
Carved in the kitchen ★ Served in thin slices ★ Broiled Medium - Medium Rare - or Rare

ORIGINAL BEEF STROGANOFF with RICE............4.25

NEW YORK SIRLOIN CUT	5.00	BROILED CALVES LIVER French Fried Onions	1.95
FILET MIGNON	4.75		
THICK HAM STEAK with Pineapple	2.25	BREADED VEAL CUTLETS Country Gravy	1.95

 NEW YORK STEAK SANDWICH............2.75

DESSERTS

Cheese Cake	.45
Assorted Pie	.35
Ice Cream	.25
Sherbet	.25

CHEESE

Roquefort	.40
Liederkranz	.40
Camembert	.40

BEVERAGES

Coffee	.20
Tea	.20
Milk	.20
Sanka or Postum	.25